100 Turn-of-the-Century Brick Bungalows
with Floor Plans

ROGERS & MANSON

DOVER PUBLICATIONS, INC.

NEW YORK

Copyright

Published in Canada by General Publishing Company, Ltd., 30 Lesmill Road, Don Mills, Toronto, Ontario.

Published in the United Kingdom by Constable and Company, Ltd., 3 The Lanchesters, 162–164 Fulham Palace Road, London W6 9ER.

Bibliographical Note

This Dover edition, first published in 1994, is an unabridged republication of *One Hundred Bungalows*, originally published for The Building Brick Association of America by Rogers & Manson, Boston, in 1912.

Library of Congress Cataloging-in-Publication Data

100 turn-of-the-century brick bungalows with floor plans.
    p.   cm.
    "An unabridged republication of One hundred bungalows, originally published for the Building Brick Association of America, by Rogers & Manson, Boston, in 1912"—T.p. verso.
    ISBN 0-486-28119-1
    1. Bungalows—United States—Designs and plans. 2. Brick houses—United States—Designs and plans. I. One hundred bungalows. II. Title: One hundred turn-of-the-century brick bungalows with floor plans.
NA7571.A14 1994
728′.373—dc20
                                         94-6540
                                         CIP

Manufactured in the United States of America
Dover Publications, Inc., 31 East 2nd Street, Mineola, N.Y. 11501

ONE HUNDRED BUNGALOWS

[Original cover]

One Hundred Bungalows

FOREWORD

THE Bungalow Designs which are illustrated in this book have been selected from 666 drawings submitted by architects and draughtsmen from all parts of the country, in a competition recently conducted by the *Brickbuilder*.

The subject of this competition was a brick bungalow to be built complete—exclusive of the land—for $3000. The three prize designs, the eight "honorable mention" designs and most of the others here published can, in the opinion of competent authorities, be built of good wholesome materials for this figure; a few of the designs would cost somewhat more.

It is interesting to note that the program called for "bungalow designs;" the results as set forth in this book therefore fairly represent the interpretation of the word "bungalow" on the part of a large number of the architectural profession.

One naturally associates the word "bungalow" with a type of dwelling which had its origin in India and which has been reproduced, with modifications, in California, through the mountains of our middle country and by the sea. The original bungalow was of one story; all the rooms being on the ground floor; frequently houses of this type were built partly or wholly around an open square or patio. With characteristic disregard for precedent, however, we seem to have arrived at the conclusion that a house of one story or of one story and a half — heretofore known as a cottage — may properly be classed as a bungalow. Since the dignity of the small house will not suffer by this designation, there can be no good reason why we should not accept the designs herein shown as fairly representative of the modern American bungalow.

What we most need in America is a better class of small domestic architecture, one which shall provide us with houses more wholesome in their external appearance and more satisfying in their internal arrangement and finish.

The one notable feature in connection with home building today is the interest everywhere manifested, in the fundamentals which insure a good house. These may be set down as style, plan and the materials of construction.

In order to secure style — and by this we mean those external forms which, even though simple, are refined — that shall reflect the best practice of our time, no better receipt can be given than — go to a good architect. The same source will supply the needed help for the arrangement of the plan.

As to materials of which to build the house, there is nothing which will give it so much dignity, stability and permanency as Brick — but of this we shall have more to say in the following pages.

No attempt has been made in this book to arrange the designs, following those which were given Prizes and Mentions, in the order of their merit.

DETAIL OF FIRST PRIZE DESIGN BUNGALOW SUBMITTED IN THE BRICK-
BUILDER COMPETITION AND BUILT AT THE COLISEUM, CHICAGO.

Ralph J. Batchelder, Architect.

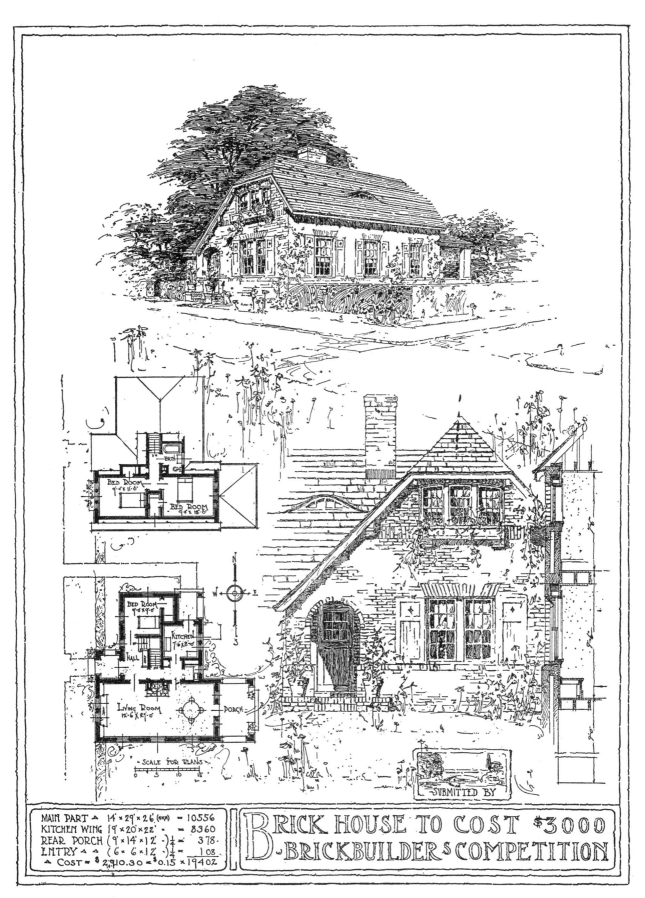

MAIN PART — 14' × 29' × 26' (HIGH) — 10556
KITCHEN WING 19' × 20' × 22' — 8360
REAR PORCH (9' × 14' × 12')¼ — 378.
ENTRY (6' × 6' × 12')¼ — 108
COST = $2,910.30 = $0.15 × 19402

BRICK HOUSE TO COST $3000
BRICKBUILDERS COMPETITION

AWARDED FIRST PRIZE
DESIGN BY RALPH J. BATCHELDER
40 Central Street, Boston, Mass.

5

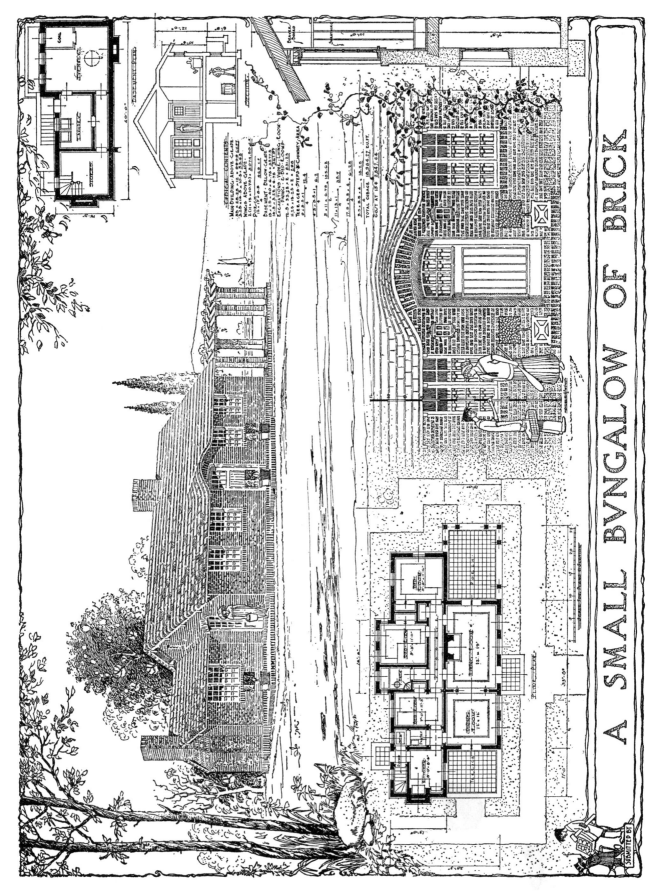

A SMALL BVNGALOW OF BRICK

6

·SCALE OF PLANS·

FIRST FLOOR PLAN

SECOND FLOOR PLAN

SVBMITTED BY

CVBAGE IS FIGVRED
IN THREE SECTIONS
VERANDA ¼ OF 8 BY
32.5 BY 14 = 910. CV.FT
LIVING RM PORTION

14.5 BY 32.5 BY 27 FT IN
HEIGHT = 12,723.75
HALL· KITCHEN AND
BED RM 9.75 BY 32.5
BY 21 FT = 6657 FT

SVBTRACTING 300
FOR VNEXCAVATED
PART VNDER BED RM

MAKES TOTAL 19990

VERANDA

LIVING ROOM

KITCHEN   HALL   BED ROOM

BED RM   BATH   BED ROOM

COMPETITION FOR A SMALL HOVSE
OF THE BVNGALOW TYPE

AWARDED THIRD PRIZE
DESIGN BY WILLIAM BOYD, JR.
323 4th Avenue, Pittsburgh, Pa.

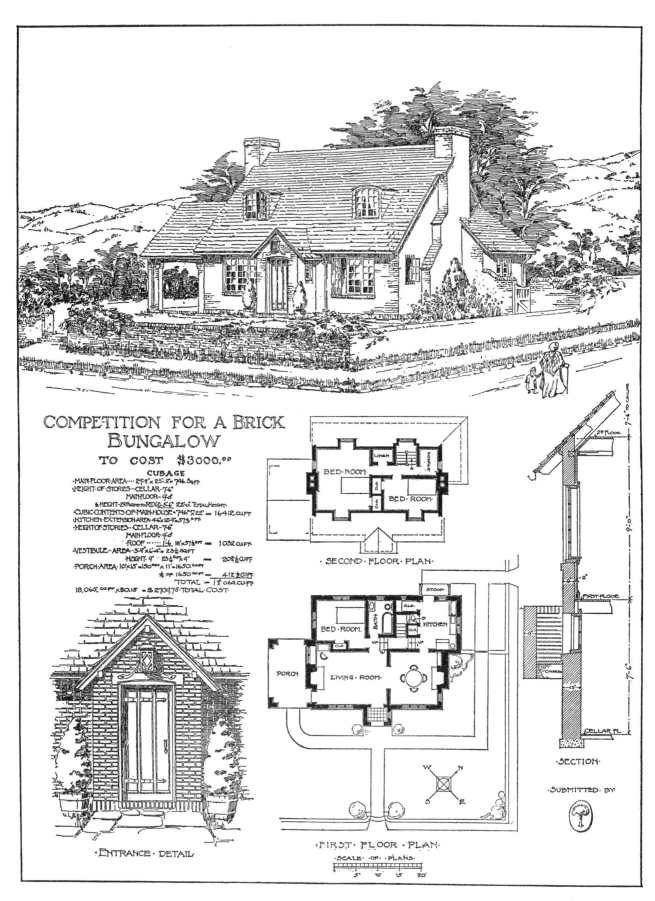

COMPETITION FOR A BRICK BUNGALOW

TO COST $3000.00

CUBAGE

·MAIN·FLOOR·AREA··· 29'-8"x 25'-2" 746.5q.FT
·HEIGHT·OF·STORIES··CELLAR· 7'-6"
MAIN·FLOOR· 9'-8"
½·HEIGHT· 29'-6" to RIDGE· 5'-6" 22'-0. TotalHeight.
·CUBIC·CONTENTS·OF·MAIN·HOUSE· 746"x22" 16412.CU.FT.
·KITCHEN·EXTENSION·AREA· 4-6x12-9. 573.5q.FT.
·HEIGHT·OF·STORIES···CELLAR· 7'-6"
MAIN·FLOOR· 9'-8"
·ROOF ····· 1-6" 18'x57½sq.ft 1032.CU.FT.
VESTIBULE··AREA·· 3'-9"x6'-4" 23½5q.FT.
HEIGHT· 9' 23½sq.ft x 9' 208½ CU.FT.
·PORCH·AREA· 10'x15" 150sq.ft x 11" 1650.CU.FT.
½ of 1650.CU.FT. 412½CU.FT.
TOTAL 18,065.CU.FT.
18,065. CU.FT. x 30.15 = $2704.75.TOTAL·COST·

·SECOND·FLOOR·PLAN·

BED·ROOM   LINEN   STORES
          BED·ROOM

·ENTRANCE·DETAIL·

·FIRST·FLOOR·PLAN·

STOOP
BED·ROOM.   BATH   KITCHEN   CLO.
CLO.   UP   UP
PORCH   LIVING·ROOM.

·SCALE·OF·PLANS·
5' 10' 15' 20'

·SECTION·

·SUBMITTED·BY·

AWARDED FOURTH PRIZE
DESIGN BY CHARLES WILLING
Provident Building, 4th and Chestnut Streets, Philadelphia, Pa.

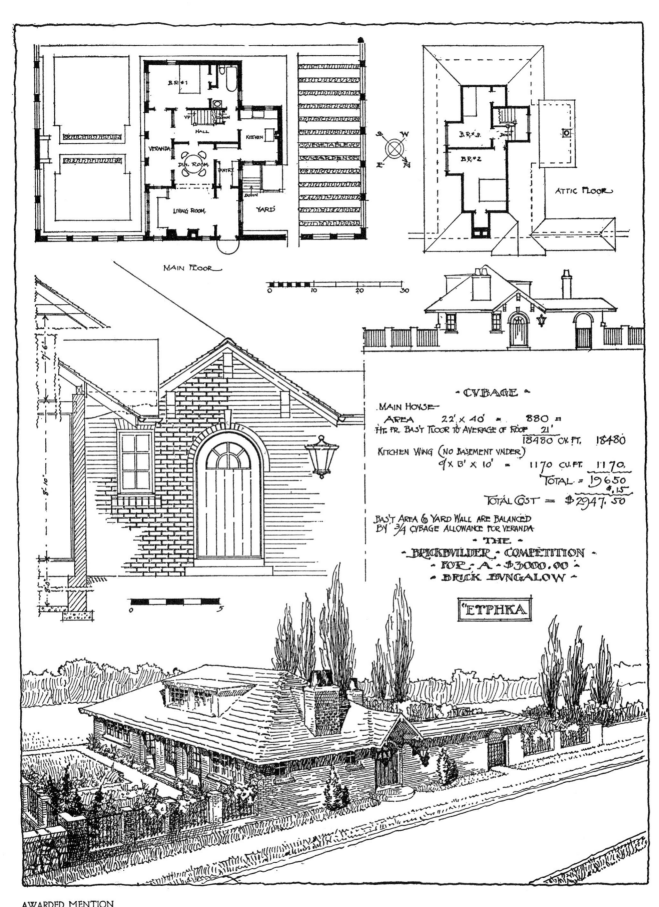

MAIN FLOOR

ATTIC FLOOR

- CVBAGE -

MAIN HOVSE
AREA   22' x 40' =   880 ﬩
HT. FR. BAS'T FLOOR TO AVERAGE OF ROOF   21'
18480 CV. FT.   18480
KITCHEN WING (NO BASEMENT VNDER)
9' x 13' x 10' =   1170 CV.FT.   1170.
TOTAL = 19650
TOTAL COST = $2947.50

BAS'T AREA & YARD WALL ARE BALANCED
BY ¾ CVBAGE ALLOWANCE FOR VERANDA

- THE -
- BRICKBVILDER · COMPETITION -
- FOR · A · $3000.00 -
- BRICK · BVNGALOW -

"ETPHKA"

AWARDED MENTION
DESIGN BY HARRIS ALLEN
2514 Hillegass Avenue, Berkeley, Cal.

9

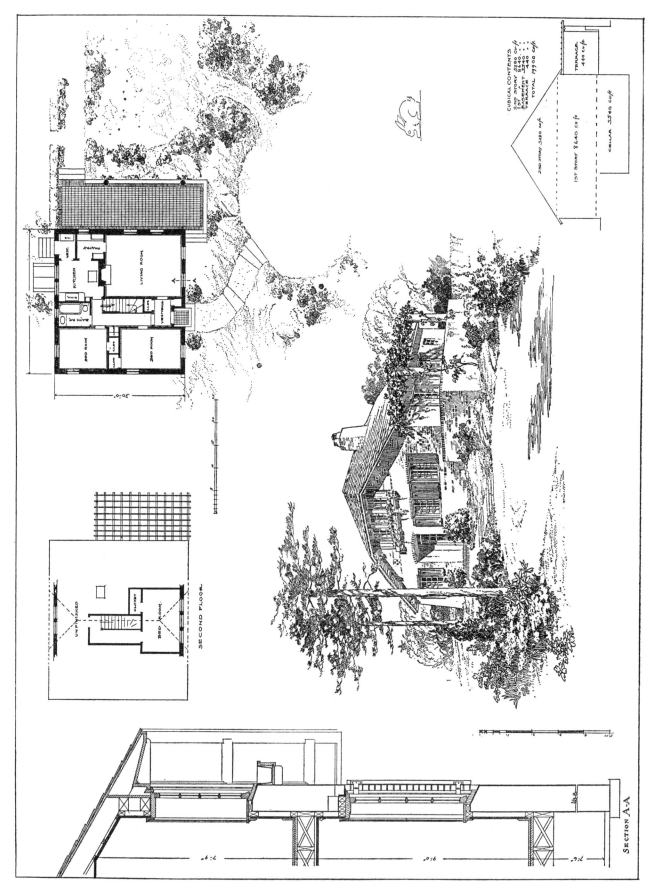

AWARDED MENTION
DESIGN BY ADDISON B. LE BOUTILLIER

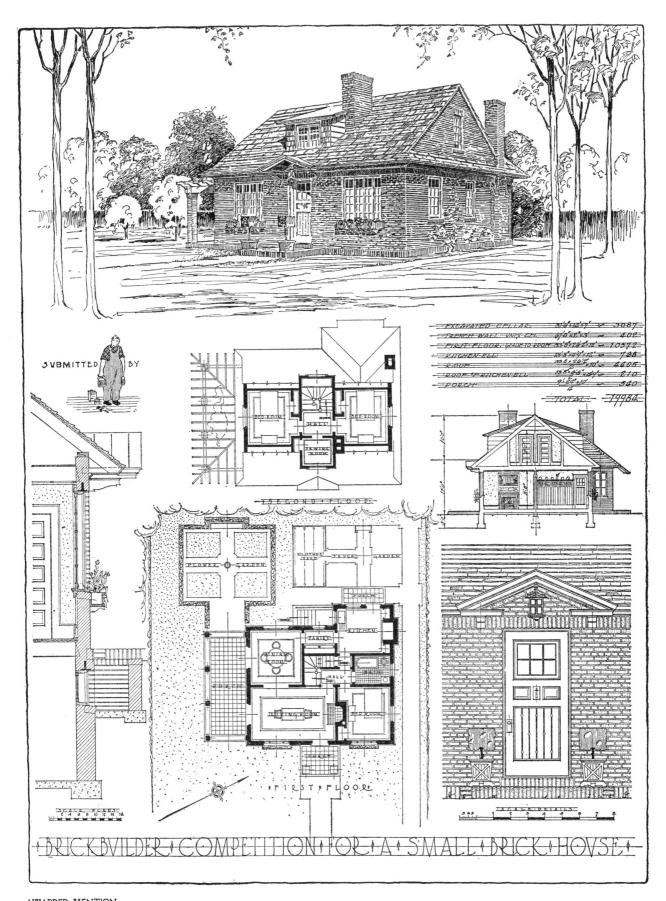

SUBMITTED BY

EXCAVATED CELLAR

TRENCH WALL

FIRST FLOOR

KITCHEN-ELL

ROOF

ROOF & KITCHEN-ELL

PORCH

TOTAL

SECOND FLOOR

FLOWER GARDEN

CLOTHES YARD   TRUCK   GARDEN

PORCH

DINING ROOM

PANTRY

KITCHEN

HALL

BATH

LIVING ROOM

BED ROOM

FIRST FLOOR

BRICKBVILDER COMPETITION FOR A SMALL BRICK HOVSE

AWARDED MENTION
DESIGN BY HENRY JAY BRIGGS
Apartment 102, The Eckington, Washington, D. C.

11

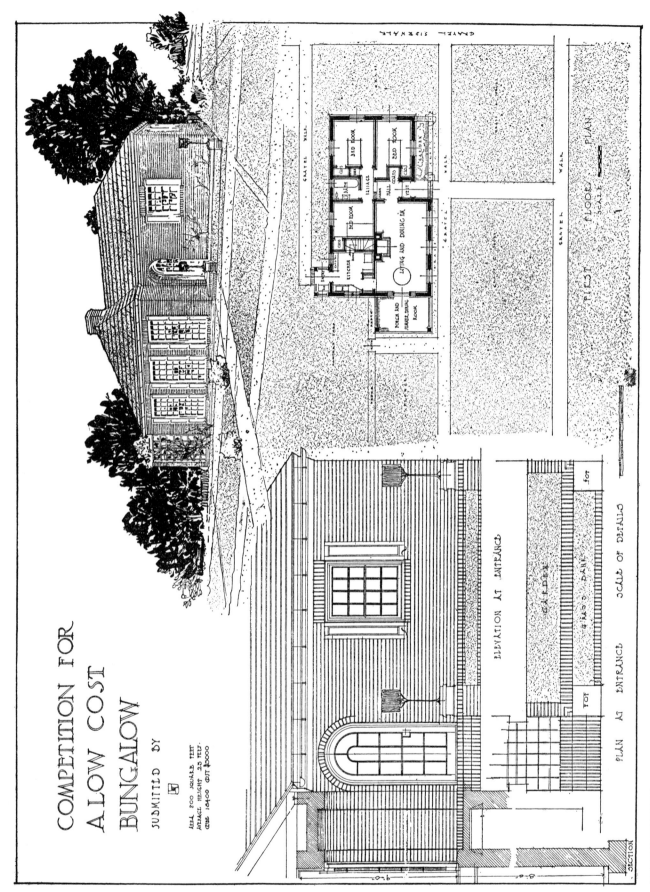

COMPETITION FOR A LOW COST BUNGALOW

SUBMITTED BY

AWARDED MENTION
DESIGN BY F. D. BULMAN
31 Beacon Street, Boston, Mass.

12

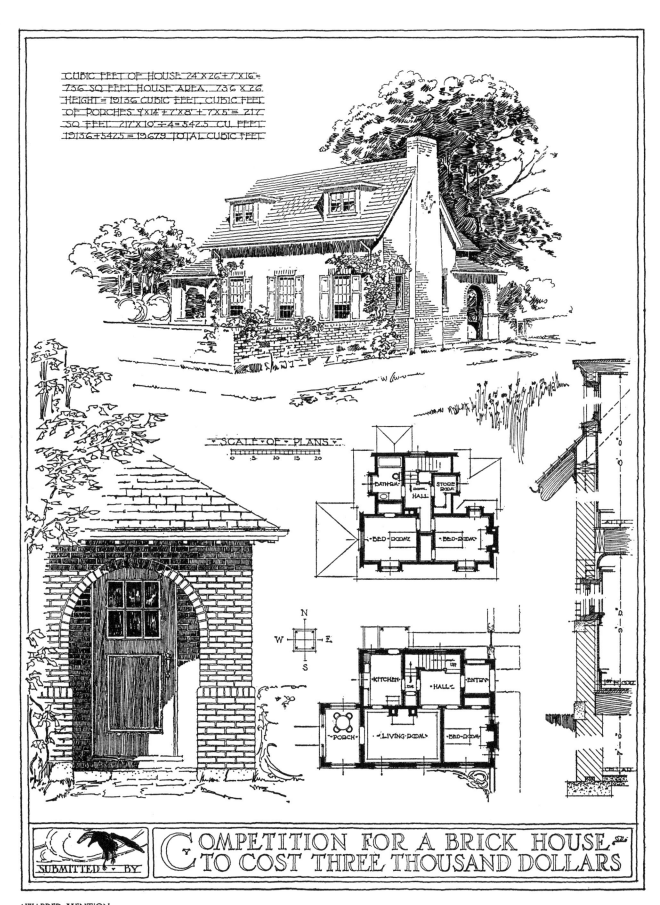

CUBIC FEET OF HOUSE 24'X26'+7'X16' =
736 SQ FEET HOUSE AREA. 736 X 26
HEIGHT = 19136 CUBIC FEET. CUBIC FEET
OF PORCHES 9'X14'+7'X8'+7'X5' = 217
SQ FEET. 217 X10 ÷4 = 542.5 CU FEET
19136+5425 = 19678 TOTAL CUBIC FEET

SCALE OF PLANS

BATH·RM   STOR·
           HALL ROOM

·BED·ROOM·   ·BED·ROOM·

N
W   E
S

KITCHEN   HALL   ENTRY

·PORCH· ·LIVING·ROOM· ·BED·ROOM·

COMPETITION FOR A BRICK HOUSE
TO COST THREE THOUSAND DOLLARS

SUBMITTED · BY

AWARDED MENTION
DESIGN BY J. MARTIN BROWN
514 West 184th Street, New York, N. Y.

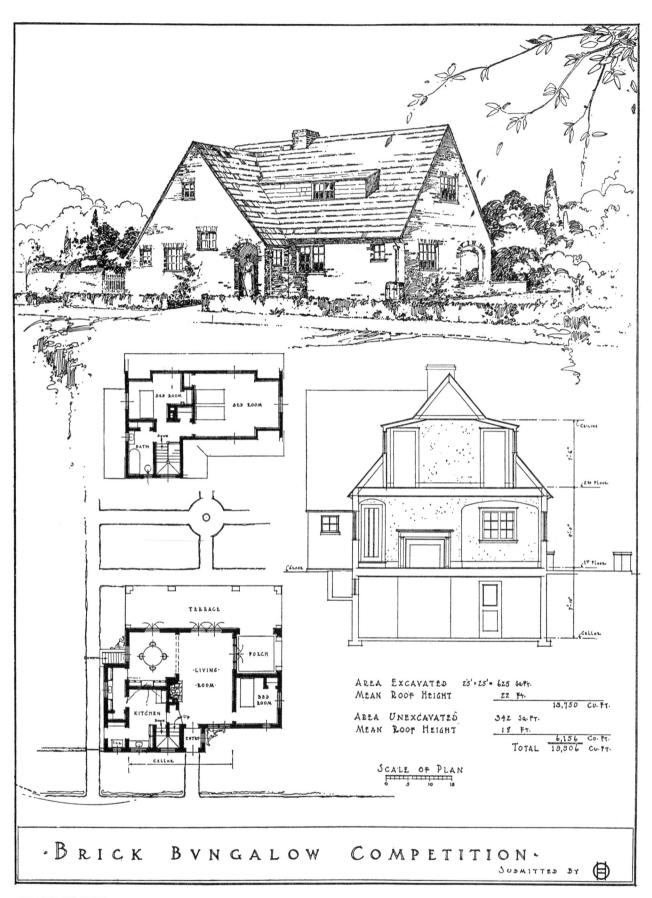

AREA EXCAVATED   25'×25'= 625 Sq.Ft.
MEAN ROOF HEIGHT   22 Ft.
                                    13,750 Cu.Ft.
AREA UNEXCAVATED   342 Sq.Ft.
MEAN ROOF HEIGHT   18 Ft.
                                     6,156 Cu.Ft.
                    TOTAL   19,906 Cu.Ft.

SCALE OF PLAN
0   5   10   15

·BRICK BVNGALOW COMPETITION·
SVBMITTED BY

AWARDED MENTION
DESIGN BY CLINTON HALL
630 Belvidere Avenue, Plainfield, N. J.

14

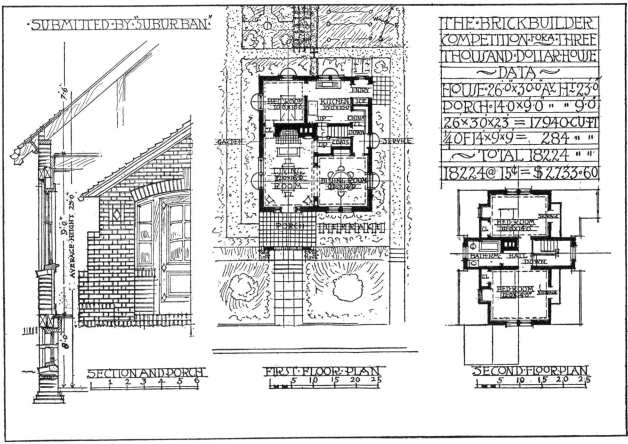

AWARDED MENTION
DESIGN BY EDWARD F. MAHER
100 Boylston Street, Room 624, Boston, Mass.

15

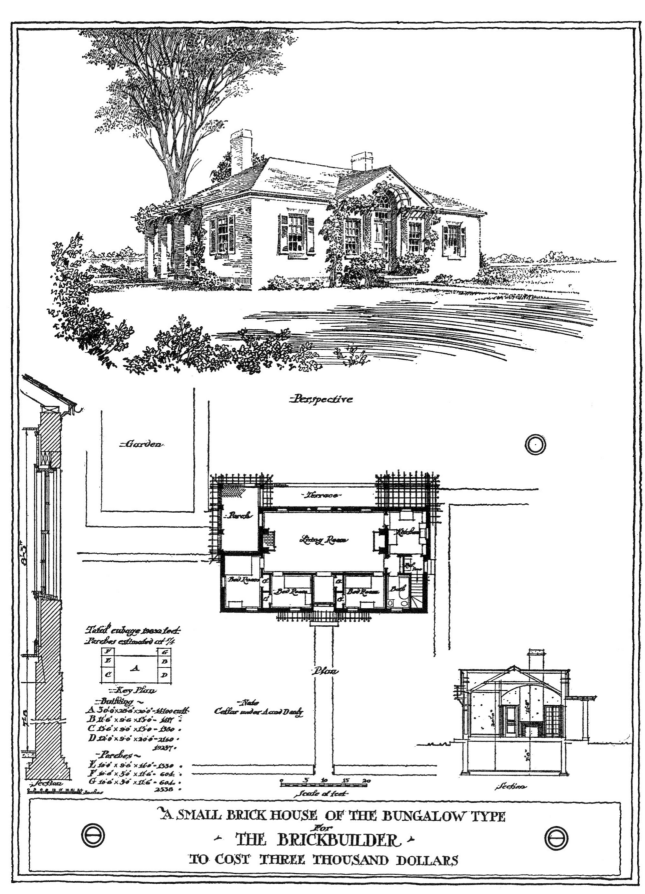

Perspective

A SMALL BRICK HOUSE OF THE BUNGALOW TYPE
for
THE BRICKBUILDER
TO COST THREE THOUSAND DOLLARS

AWARDED MENTION
DESIGN BY ALFRED COAKMAN CASS
77 Washington Place, New York, N. Y.

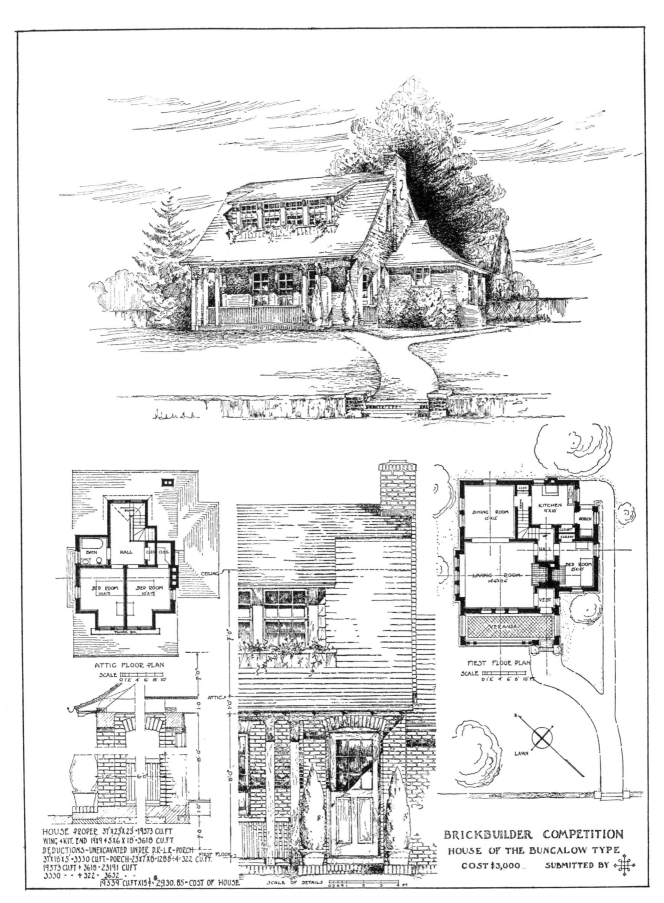

ATTIC FLOOR PLAN
SCALE

FIRST FLOOR PLAN
SCALE

HOUSE PROPER 37'X23'X23' = 19,573 CU.FT
WING + KIT. END 19'X9' + 5X6 X 18' = 3618 CU.FT
DEDUCTIONS = UNEXCAVATED UNDER D.R. + L.R. + PORCH =
37'X18'X5' = 3330 CU.FT + PORCH = 23'X7'X8' = 1288 + 4 = 322 CU.FT.
19,573 CU.FT + 3618 = 23,191 CU.FT
3330 = - + 322 = 3652
19,539 CU.FT X 15¢ = 2,930.85 = COST OF HOUSE

SCALE OF DETAILS

BRICKBUILDER COMPETITION
HOUSE OF THE BUNGALOW TYPE
COST $3,000   SUBMITTED BY

DESIGN BY JOHN C. DODD
430 Valley Road, Upper Montclair, N. J.

DESIGN BY CHARLES SUMNER SCHNEIDER
1109 Schofield Building, Cleveland, Ohio

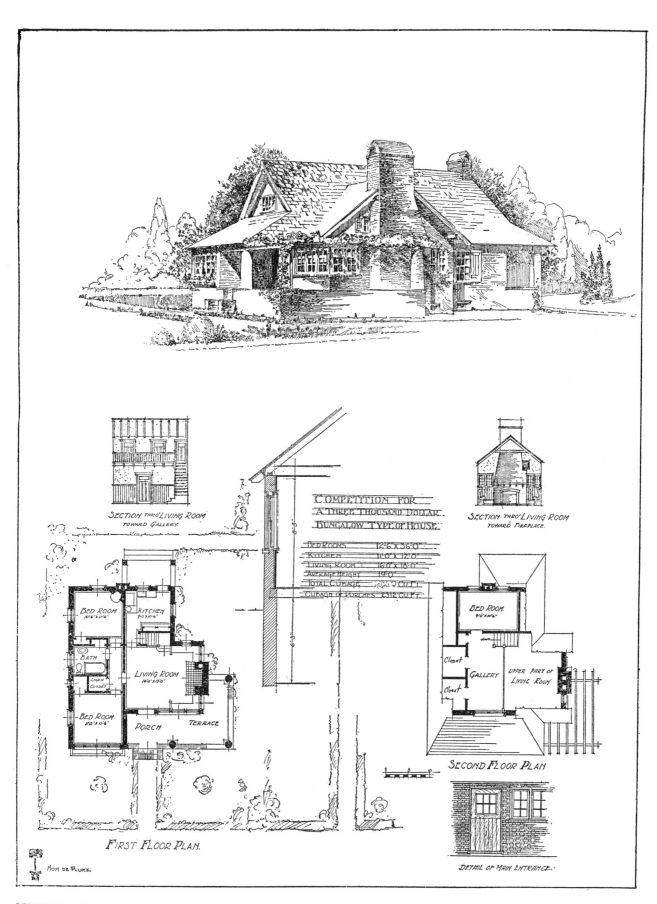

SECTION THRO' LIVING ROOM
TOWARD GALLERY.

SECTION THRO' LIVING ROOM
TOWARD FIREPLACE.

COMPETITION FOR
A THREE THOUSAND DOLLAR
BUNGALOW TYPE OF HOUSE.

BED ROOMS	12'6" X 36'0"
KITCHEN	11'0" X 12'0"
LIVING ROOM	16'0" X 18'0"
AVERAGE HEIGHT	19'0"
TOTAL CUBAGE	CU. FT.
CUBAGE OF PORCHES	2312 CU. FT.

BED ROOM
10'6" X 11'0"

KITCHEN
11'0" X 12'0"

BATH

LINEN
CLOSET

LIVING ROOM
14'0" X 17'0"

BED ROOM
11'0" X 11'6"

PORCH

TERRACE

FIRST FLOOR PLAN.

BED ROOM
9'0" X 11'6"

Closet

Closet

GALLERY

UPPER PART OF
LIVING ROOM

SECOND FLOOR PLAN.

DETAIL OF MAIN ENTRANCE.

NOM DE PLUME.

DESIGN BY ANTON A. LETZGUS
1218 Chestnut Street, Philadelphia, Pa.

·A·BUNGALOW·OF·BRICK·
·BRICKBUILDER·COMPETITION·
·SUBMITTED·BY·

·FIRST·FLOOR·PLAN·

·ALCOVE·

·SECTION·THRO'·WALL·
·SCALE: ¼"=1'-0"·

·SCALE·OF·PLAN·

FRONTAGE	DEPTH	HEIGHT	TOTAL CU·FT·
46'-0"	X 29'-0" X	12'-6" =	16675
38'-0"	X 14'-8" X	8'-0" =	4463
			21138
142 sq·ft x ¾	X	12'-6" =	1332
			19806 CU·FT·

19806 cu·ft· @ 15ᶜ per ft = $2970·90

DESIGN BY WILLIAM F. GOODRICH
310 Sun Building, Detroit, Mich.

20

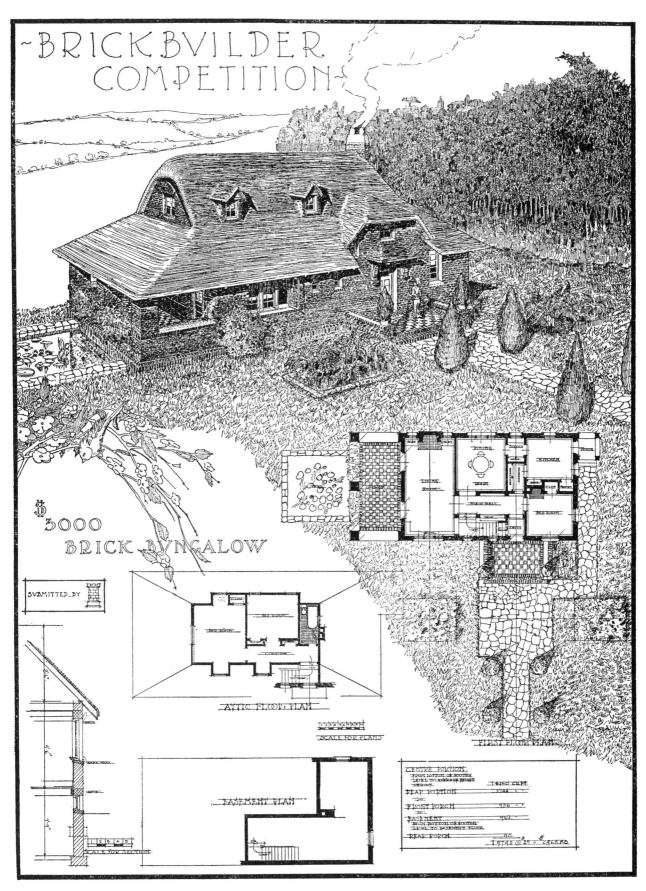

~BRICKBVILDER
COMPETITION~

$3000
BRICK BVNGALOW

SVBMITTED BY

ATTIC FLOOR PLAN

SCALE FOR PLANS

FIRST FLOOR PLAN

SCALE FOR SECTION

BASEMENT PLAN

DESIGN BY E. R. JAMES
632 Candler Building, Atlanta, Ga.

21

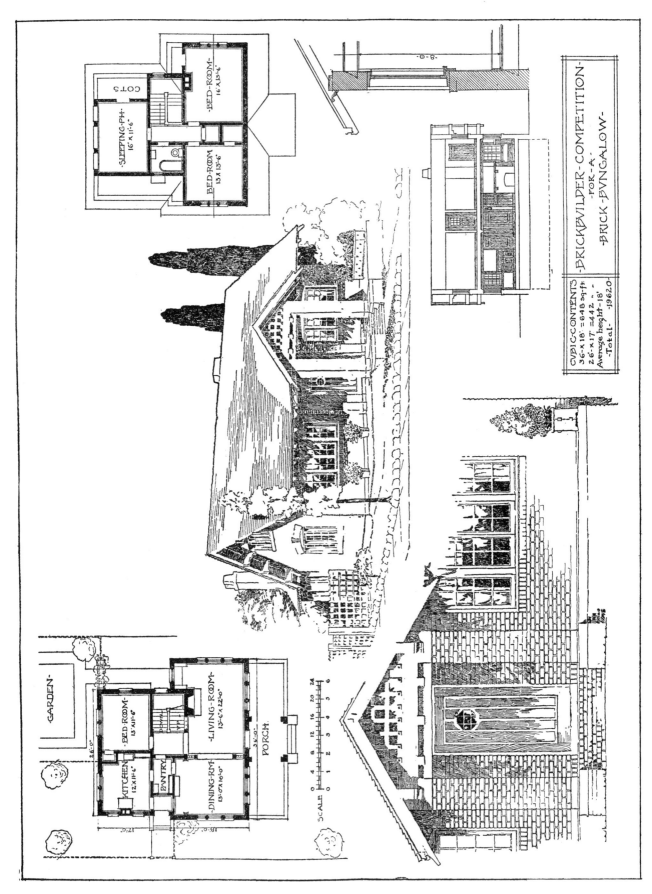

SLEEPING · P.H·
16' X 11'-6"

COTS

BED·ROOM·
16' X 15'-6"

BED·ROOM·
13' X 15'-6"

·BRICKBVILDER · COMPETITION·
·FOR · A·
·BRICK · BVNGALOW·

CVBIC·CONTENTS
36' X 18' = 648 sq·ft·
26' X 17' = 442 " "
Average height · 18'
·Total · · 19620·

·GARDEN·

BED·ROOM·
13' X 11'-6"

KITCHEN
12' X 11'-6"

PANTRY

·DINING·RM·
13'-6" X 16'-0"

·LIVING·ROOM·
13'-6" X 22'-0"

·PORCH·

SCALE   0 4 8 12 16 20 24
         0 1 2 3 4 5 6

DESIGN BY A. N. TORBITT
Springfield, Mo.

22

DETAIL

0 1 2 3 4

FIRST FLOOR PLAN

01 5 10 12
SCALE

SECTION

SCALE

CHAMBER BATH CHAMBER

KITCHEN CHAMBER

DINING LIVING ROOM

NOTE
DOTTED LINES
SHOW PORTABLE
SCREEN TO BE
USED WHEN
DINING

30'-0"

0'-6"

7'-0"

ESTIMATE OF COST
PART WITH BASEMENT
  29'-6 X 25'-0 X 19'-6 = 14381.25 CU·FT
PART WHERE UNEXCAVATED
  29'-6 X 14'-0 X 12'-0 = 4,956. CU·FT
PERGOLA
  (29'-6 X 9'-0 X 9'-0)¼ = 597.37 CU·FT
TOTAL   19,934.62 CU·FT
PRICE PER CUBIC FOOT 15¢
COST OF BUNGALOW $2,990.19

BRICK ~ BUNGALOW
BRICKBUILDER ~ COMPETITION

SUBMITTED BY

DESIGN BY ADRIAN CLARK FINLAYSON
614 Quincy Street, Washington, D. C.

23

COMPETITION FOR A $3000 BRICK HOUSE

SUBMITTED BY

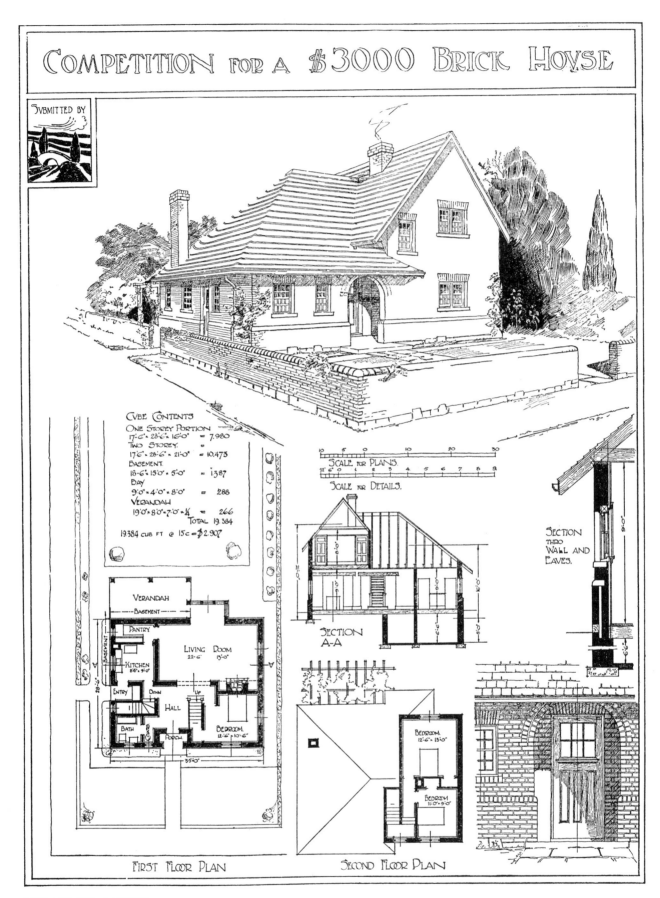

CUBE CONTENTS
ONE STOREY PORTION
17'-6" × 28'-6" × 16'-0" = 7.980
TWO STOREY.
17'-6" × 28'-6" × 21'-0" = 10.473
BASEMENT.
18'-6" × 15'-0" × 5'-0" = 1.387
BAY
9'-0" × 4'-0" × 8'-0" = 288
VERANDAH
19'-0" × 8'-0" × 7'-0" × ½ = 266
TOTAL 19.384

19.384 CUB FT @ 15c = $2.907

SCALE FOR PLANS.

SCALE FOR DETAILS.

SECTION THRO WALL AND EAVES.

SECTION A-A

VERANDAH
BASEMENT
PANTRY
KITCHEN 8'6" × 9'-0"
LIVING ROOM 22'-6" × 15'-0"
ENTRY
DOWN
UP
HALL
BATH
PORCH
BEDROOM 12'-6" × 10'-6"

FIRST FLOOR PLAN

BEDROOM 12'-6" × 13'-0"
BEDROOM 11'-0" × 9'-0"

SECOND FLOOR PLAN

DESIGN BY GEO. E. HEDLEY
20 Alvin Avenue, Toronto, Ont., Can.

24

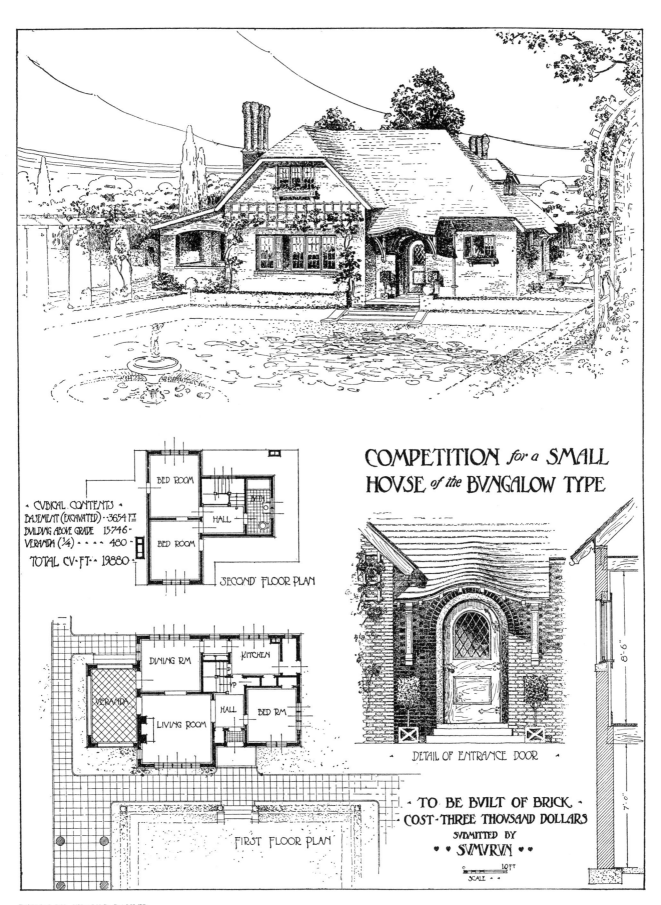

COMPETITION *for a* **SMALL HOVSE** *of the* **BVNGALOW TYPE**

· CVBICAL · CONTENTS ·
BASEMENT (EXCAVATED) · 3654 FT
BVILDVG ABOVE GRADE · 15746 ·
VERANDA (¼) · · · · 480 ·
TOTAL CV · FT · 19880 ·

SECOND FLOOR PLAN

BED ROOM
HALL
MIN
BED ROOM

DINING RM
KITCHEN
VERANDA
LIVING ROOM
HALL
BED RM

FIRST FLOOR PLAN

DETAIL OF ENTRANCE DOOR

· TO · BE · BVILT · OF · BRICK ·
· COST · THREE · THOVSAND · DOLLARS ·
SVBMITTED BY
♥ ♥ SVMVRVN ♥ ♥

10 FT
SCALE

8'-6"
7'-0"

DESIGN BY JERAULD DAHLER
611 W. 127th Street, New York, N. Y.

25

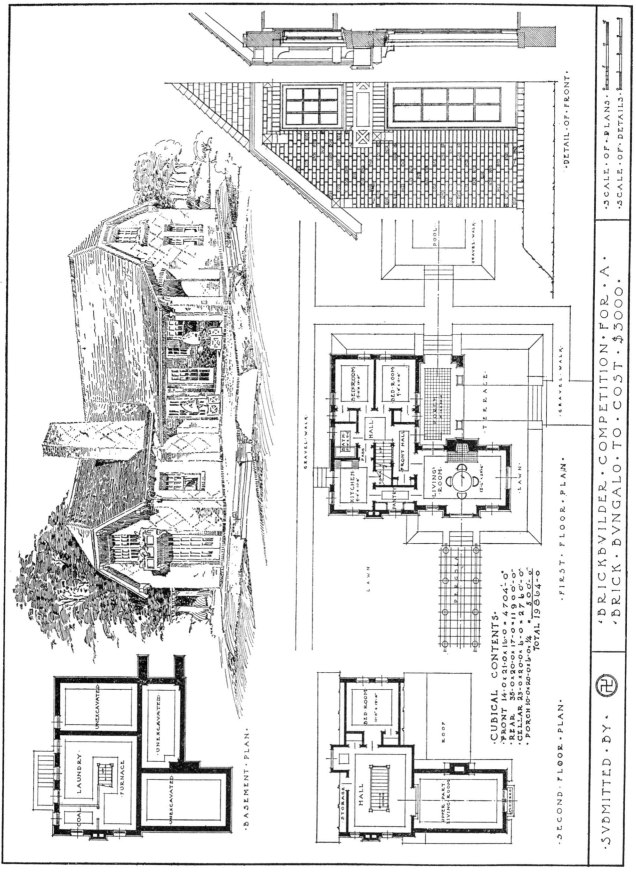

CUBICAL CONTENTS.
FRONT 14·0×21·0×16·0 = 4704·0
REAR 35·0×20·0·17·0 = 11900·0
CELLAR 23·0×30·0×6·0 = 2760·0
PORCH 10·0×20·0·0·1/4 = 500·0
TOTAL 19864·0

·SECOND·FLOOR·PLAN·

·BASEMENT·PLAN·

·FIRST·FLOOR·PLAN·

·DETAIL·OF·FRONT·

·SCALE·OF·PLANS·

·SCALE·OF·DETAILS·

·SVBMITTED·BY· ⌂ ·BRICKBVILDER·COMPETITION·FOR·A·
·BRICK·BVNGALO·TO·COST·$3000.

DESIGN BY JOHN M. MARRIOTT
20 East Broad Street, Columbus, Ohio

26

33'x23½'=775□'+13x6=853.□'·TOT·AREA·
AVERAGE HEIGHT 23'· CUBE OF
HOUSE 19619· CUBE OF PORCH.
¼·7x20x10=350· TOTALCUBE 19969.

BED ROOM
12 x 12

BED ROOM
12x15·6·

0   5   10   15   20
FT.

BED ROOM
12 x 10·6·

BATH

KITCHEN
9x10·6·

LIVING ROOM
11 x18·6·

DINING RM
11 x 12·

ALCOVE
5 x 12·

PORCH

BRICKBUILDER COMPETITION FOR A BRICK BUNGALOW TO COST THREE THOUSAND DOLLARS

DESIGN BY STEWARD WAGNER
40 W. 36th Street, New York, N. Y.

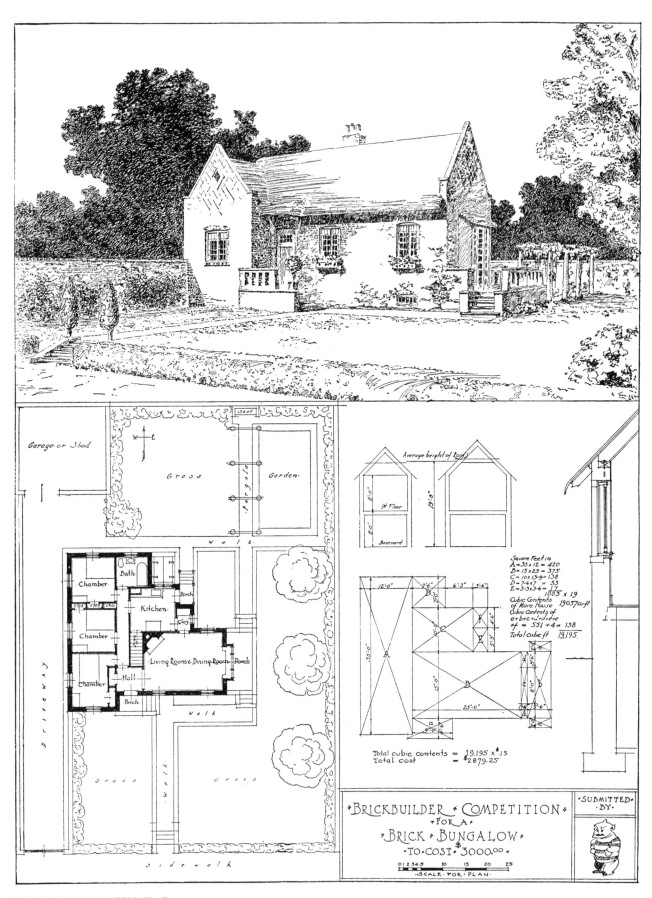

DESIGN BY FRANK H. COLONY, JR.
408 Board of Education, St. Louis, Mo.

28

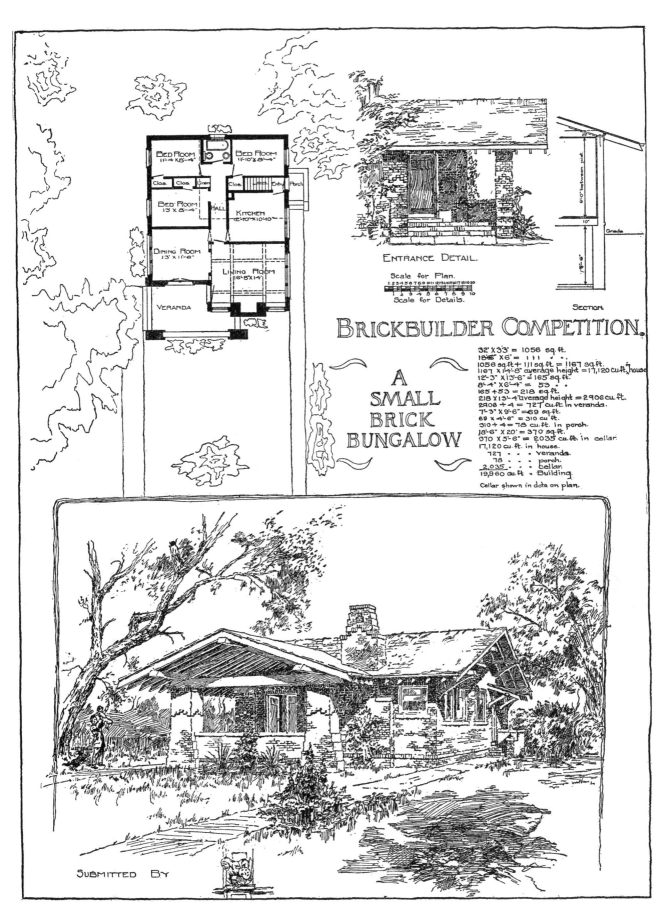

ENTRANCE DETAIL.

Scale for Plan.

Scale for Details.

SECTION.

BRICKBUILDER COMPETITION.

A
SMALL
BRICK
BUNGALOW

32' X 33' = 1056 sq. ft.
18'6" X 6' = 111 "
1056 sq. ft + 111 sq. ft = 1167 sq. ft.
1167 X 14'-8" average height = 17,120 cu. ft. house
12'-3" X 13'-6" = 165 sq. ft.
8'-4" X 6'-4" = 53 "
165 + 53 = 218 sq. ft.
218 X 13'-4" average height = 2906 cu. ft.
2906 ÷ 4 = 727 cu. ft. in veranda.
7'-3" X 9'-6" = 69 sq. ft.
69 X 4'-6" = 310 cu. ft.
310 ÷ 4 = 78 cu. ft. in porch.
18'-6" X 20' = 370 sq. ft.
370 X 5'-6" = 2035 cu. ft. in cellar.
17,120 cu. ft. in house.
727 " " " veranda.
78 " " " porch.
2,035 " " " cellar.
19,960 cu. ft. = Building.

Cellar shown in dots on plan.

SUBMITTED BY

DESIGN BY LEO N. DENLER
275 Mortimer Street, Buffalo, N. Y.

29

COMPETITION FOR A $3000.00 BRICK BUNGALOW

PLAN OF SECOND FLOOR
SCALE 1/8"=1'0"

BED ROOM
10'0x18'0

BED ROOM
17'0x18'0

ROOF

ROOF

CALCULATIONS

MAIN HOUSE 25'0x17'0 x 17'0 Average Height = 13,804 cu.ft.
BED ROOM WING 18'0x13'0 x 16'0 Average Height = 1944 cu.ft.
ENTRANCE PORCH 6'0x9'0 x10'0 Average = 142 cu.ft.
LIVING PORCH 10'0x20'0 x10'0 x one-fourth = 600 cu.ft.
BASEMENT 14'0x25'0x 7'0 = 2744 cu.ft.
TOTAL CUBEAGE = 19,234 cu.ft.

DETAIL OF FRONT ELEVATION .
SCALE 1/4"=1'0".

SECTION.
SCALE 1/4"=1'0"

SCALE OF PLANS.

SCALE OF DETAILS & PERSPECTIVE

SUBMITTED BY

FIRST FLOOR PLAN.
SCALE 1/8"=1'0".

KITCHEN
11'0x12'6

PANTRY

BACK PORCH

DINING
ROOM
13'0x18'0

BATH

LIVING
ROOM
15'0x27'6

BED ROOM
11'0x16'6

CLOSET

CLOSET

COATS

30

DESIGN BY W. P. R. PEMBER

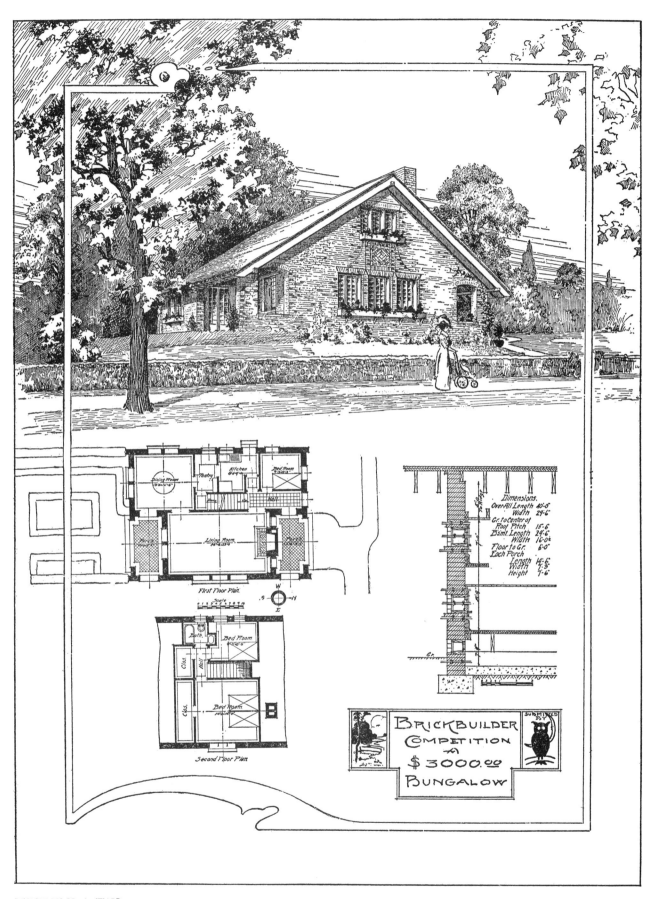

Dimensions.
Over-All Length 40'-0"
Width 29'-6"
Gr. to Center of
Roof Pitch 15'-6"
Bsmt. Length 29'-6"
Width 16'-0½"
Floor to Gr. 6'-0"
Each Porch
Length 14'-6"
Width 7'-3"
Height 7'-6"

First Floor Plan.

Second Floor Plan.

BRICKBUILDER
COMPETITION
A
$3000.00
BUNGALOW

DESIGN BY M. A. WARD
534 E. 44th Street, Chicago, Ill.

BRICKBUILDER COMPETITION FOR A SMALL HOUSE OF THE BUNGALOW TYPE SUBMITTED BY SUNNYSIDE

TABLE OF SIZES FOR CUBAGE

	CU. FT.
FRONT B'LD'G - 30'-6" x 18" x 19' HIGH =	10431
BAY WINDOWS 7'-6" x 3' x 14' HIGH x 2 =	630
REAR B'LD'G - 27'-6" x 14'-4" x 21'-6" HIGH =	8670
PORCH 13' x 7' x 11'-6" =	262
4	
TOTAL	19993

19993 CU. FT. AT 15 CTS. = $2999.00

Unfinished Unfinished

Hall

Bed Room   Clos.   Bed Room

SECOND FLOOR PLAN

Clos.

Bed Room   Kitchen   Down

Bath   Clos.   Clos.   Pantry   Coats   Dr. board

Living Room   Dining Room

Porch

FIRST FLOOR PLAN

1 2 3 4 5 6 7 8 9 10

5   10   15   20

Typical Section

8'-0"

8'-6"

3'-0"

This depth applies for Front B'ld'g only. Rear B'ld'g to have cellar 7'-6"

PART ELEVATION   PART SECTION

DESIGN BY BENJAMIN F. HENDREN
1063 Drexel Building, Philadelphia, Pa.

FIRST FLOOR PLAN

SCALE

SECOND FLOOR PLAN

COMPETITION
FOR A
SMALL HOUSE OF THE
BUNGALOW TYPE
TO BE BUILT OF BRICK

MAIN HOUSE 24 X 32 X 20 =	18560 CU. FT.	
PORCH (25%) 15 X 19 X 12 =	855	"
CHIMNEY ABOVE ROOF 5X5X2 =	50	"
BAY WINDOW 8 X 1½ X 8 =	96	"
TERRACES =	200	"
TOTAL =	19761	"

SECTION

DESIGN BY OSWALD C. HERING & DOUGLASS FITCH
1 West 34th Street, New York, N. Y.

33

A·BRICK·HOUSE·OF THE
·BUNGALOWTYPE·

·DATA·

BASEMENT	13"×26	=	338·SQ·FT.
1ST·FLOOR	26"×31"+12"×12"	=	950 " "
2ND "	26"×31"	=	806 " "
PORCHES	6"×12"+10"×13"	=	222 " "

·HEIGHTS·

FOOTINGS TO EAVES		13'-0"
1 " " BASEMENT FLOOR	4'-0"	
AVERAGE·EAVES TO RIDGE	7'-6"	

CUBAGE

BASEMENT	338×4 =	1332 CU·FT
1ST FLOOR	950×13=	10478 " "
2ND "	806×75=	6045 " "
BAY WINDOW		208 " "
PORCHES	222×17'-4"	944 " "
TOTAL		19227 " "
ALLOWABLE		20000 " "
RESERVE		773" " "

·1½" DETAIL SECTION·

·SCALE·

·FIRST FLOOR·PLAN·
·8 FEET TO THE INCH·

·SECOND FLOOR PLAN·
·8 FEET TO THE INCH·

DESIGN BY ROY A. LIPPINCOTT
907 Steinway Hall, Chicago, Ill.

COMPETITION FOR A $3,000 BUNGALOW OF BRICK

49' X 28' X 13' = 17836
BASEMENT-14X20X7.5=2,100
TOTAL 19,936
-75% OF PORCH AREA= 576
TOTAL CUBAGE 19,360

DINING ROOM · KITCHEN · BATH · BED ROOM
CHINA
LIVING ROOM · BED ROOM · BED ROOM
PORCH
PLAN

DETAIL

SUBMITTED BY

DESIGN BY MAX ALLEN VAN HOUSE
2112 F. Street, N. W., Washington, D. C.

35

COMPETITION FOR A BRICK BVNGALOW
TO COST THREE THOVSAND DOLLARS

DESIGN BY WALTER R. HAIR
705 Rentschler Building, Hamilton, Ohio

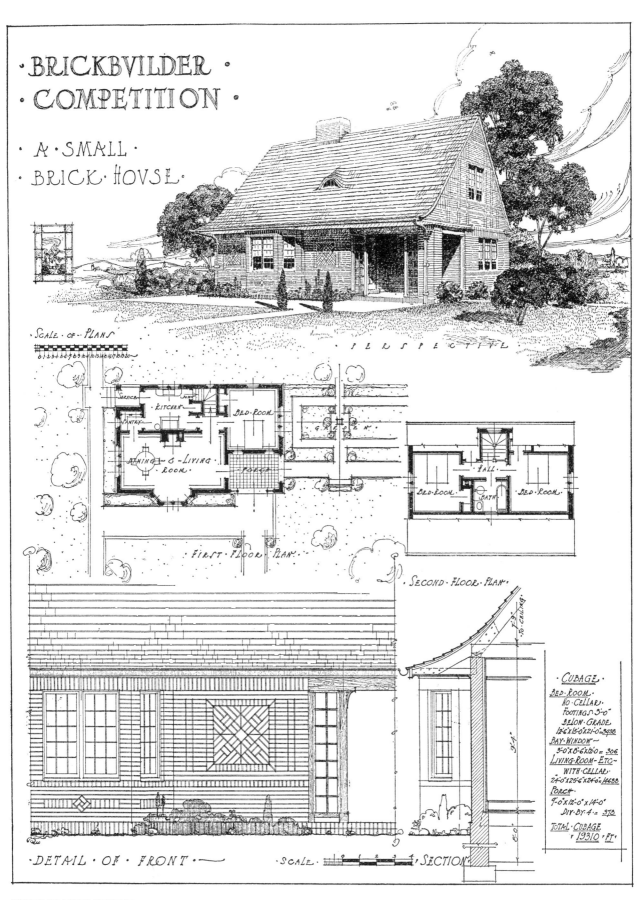

·BRICKBVILDER·
·COMPETITION·

·A·SMALL·
·BRICK·HOVSE·

PERSPECTIVE

SCALE·OF·PLANS

SERVICE
KITCHEN
PANTRY
BED·ROOM
GARDEN
DINING·&·LIVING·ROOM
PORCH

·FIRST·FLOOR·PLAN·

HALL
BED·ROOM
BATH
BED·ROOM

·SECOND·FLOOR·PLAN·

·DETAIL·OF·FRONT·—

SCALE·

·SECTION·

·CUBAGE·
·BED·ROOM·
NO·CELLAR·
FOOTINGS·3'-0"
BELOW·GRADE
12'-6"x15'-0"x21'-0"=3498
·BAY·WINDOW·—
3'-0"x8'-6"x12'-0=306
·LIVING·ROOM·ETC·
WITH·CELLAR·
24'-0"x25'-6"x24'-0"=14688
·PORCH·
7'-0"x12'-0"x14'-0"
DIV·BY·4·=·378
TOTAL·CUBAGE
·19310·FT·

DESIGN BY LEROY BARTON
479 Madison Street, Brooklyn, N. Y.

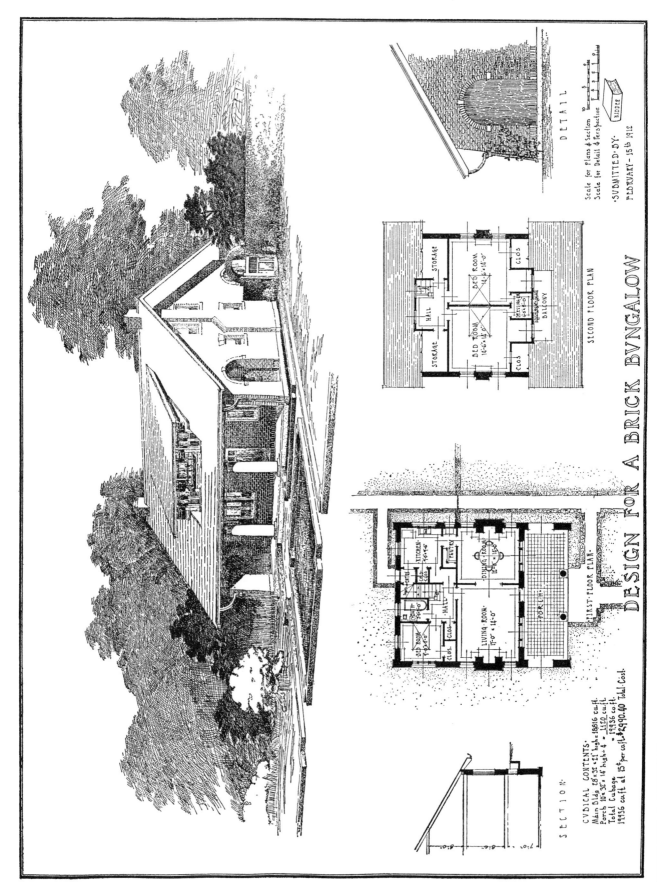

DETAIL

Scale for Plans & Section
Scale for Detail & Perspective

·SUBMITTED·BY·

FEBRUARY 15th 1912

RUDDER

SECOND FLOOR PLAN

STORAGE

HALL

BED ROOM
14'-6"x14'-0"

CLOS

STORAGE

BED ROOM
14'-6"x14'-0"

DRESSING ROOM
10'x10'-0"

BALCONY

CLOS

FIRST FLOOR PLAN

KITCHEN
16'x16'-0"

PANTRY

DINING ROOM

BED ROOM
10'-0"x14'-0"

HALL

CLOS

LIVING ROOM
17'-0"x14'-0"

PORCH

DESIGN FOR A BRICK BUNGALOW

SECTION

CUBICAL CONTENTS·
Main Bldg. 28'x38"x21' high = 18816 cu.ft.
Porch 30'x30"x 14' high = 4   = 1120 cu.ft.
Total Cubage   = 19936 cu.ft.
19936 cu.ft. at 15¢ per cu.ft.= $2990.40 Total Cost.

DESIGN BY E. C. GUTZWILLER
705 Rentschler Building, Hamilton, Ohio

38

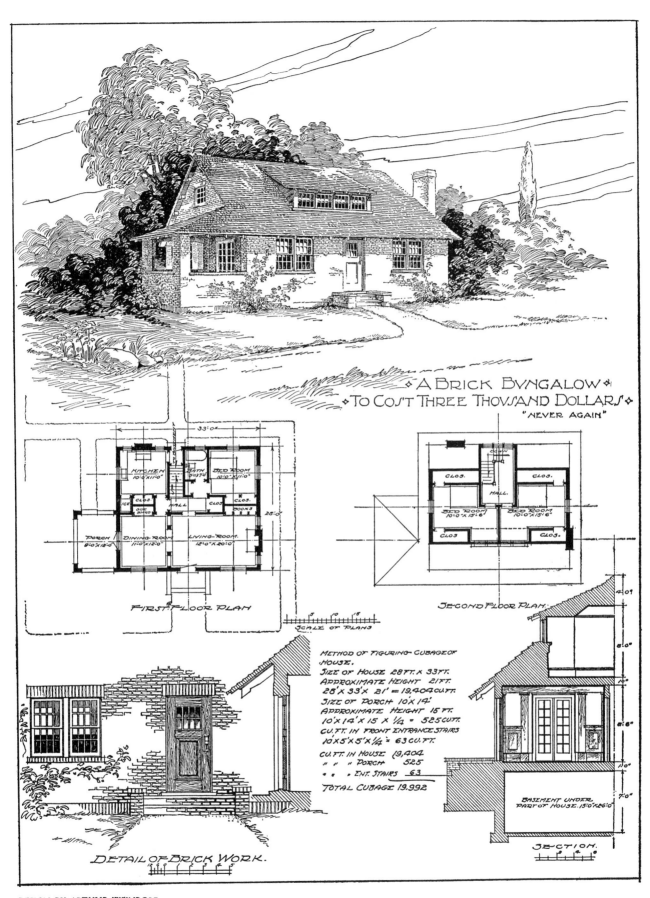

◆ A Brick Bvngalow ◆
◆ To Cost Three Thovsand Dollars ◆
"NEVER AGAIN"

FIRST FLOOR PLAN

SECOND FLOOR PLAN

SCALE OF PLANS

DETAIL OF BRICK WORK.

METHOD OF FIGURING CUBAGE OF
HOUSE.
SIZE OF HOUSE 28 FT. x 33 FT.
APPROXIMATE HEIGHT 21 FT.
28' x 33'x 21' = 19,404 CU.FT.
SIZE OF PORCH 10'x 14.'
APPROXIMATE HEIGHT 15 FT.
10'x 14'x 15 x 1/4 = 525 CU.FT.
CU. FT. IN FRONT ENTRANCE STAIRS
10'x 5'x 5'x 1/4 = 63 CU. FT.

CU. FT. IN HOUSE 19,404
  "   "   " PORCH   525
  "   "   " ENT. STAIRS   63
TOTAL CUBAGE 19,992

BASEMENT UNDER
PART OF HOUSE. 15'0"x 26'0"

SECTION.

DESIGN BY ARTHUR WEINDORF
154 Nassau Street, New York, N. Y.

39

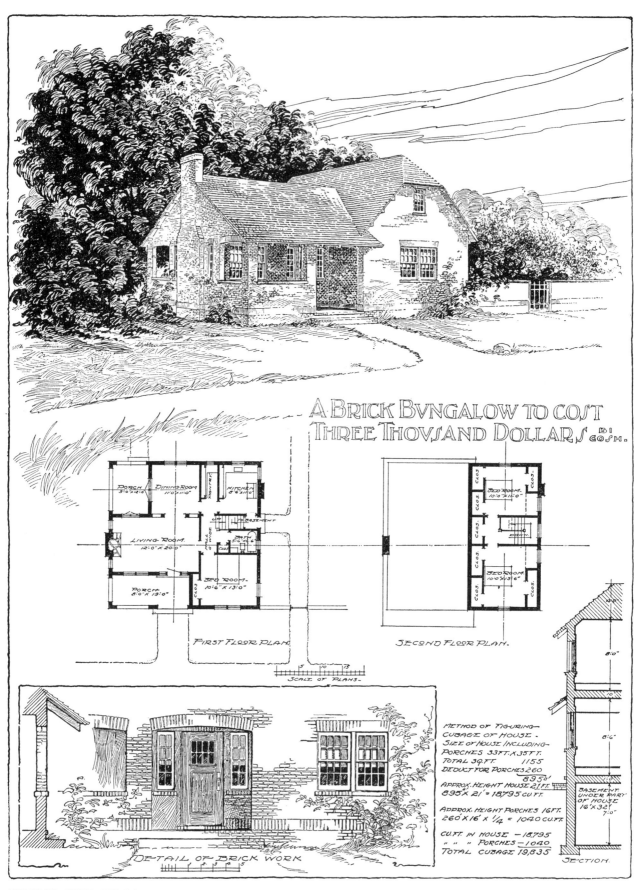

A Brick Bungalow to Cost Three Thousand Dollars by Gosh.

FIRST FLOOR PLAN.

Porch 3'6"x12'0"
Dining-Room 11'0"x11'0"
Kitchen 8'6"x11'0"
Living-Room 12'0"x20'0"
Bath 5'0"x7'6"
Bed Room 10'6"x13'0"
Porch 8'0"x19'0"
Basement

SECOND FLOOR PLAN.

Bed Room 10'0"x11'0"
Down
Bed Room 10'0"x13'6"

SCALE OF PLANS.

DETAIL OF BRICK WORK

METHOD OF FIGURING
CUBAGE OF HOUSE.
SIZE OF HOUSE INCLUDING
PORCHES 33FT.X35FT.
TOTAL SQ.FT.   1155
DEDUCT FOR PORCHES 260
                    895'
APPROX. HEIGHT HOUSE 21 FT.
895 X 21' = 18,795 CU.FT.

APPROX. HEIGHT PORCHES 16 FT.
260'X16'X 1/4 = 1040 CU.FT.

CU.FT. IN HOUSE — 18,795
 "   " PORCHES — 1040
TOTAL CUBAGE 19,835

BASEMENT
UNDER PART
OF HOUSE
16'X32'
7'0"

SECTION.

DESIGN BY ARTHUR WEINDORF
East Avenue, Long Island City, N. Y.

40

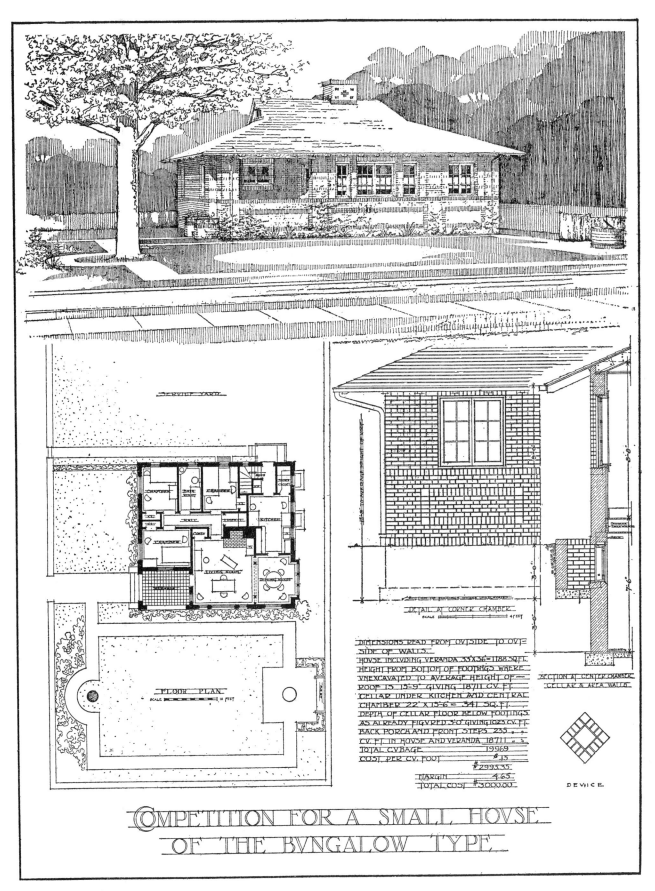

DIMENSIONS READ FROM OVTSIDE TO OVT=
SIDE OF WALLS.
HOVSE INCLVDING VERANDA 33X36=1188 SQ.FT.
HEIGHT FROM BOTTOM OF FOOTINGS WHERE
VNEXCAVATED TO AVERAGE HEIGHT OF
ROOF IS 15-9" GIVING 18711 CV. FT.
CELLAR UNDER KITCHEN AND CENTRAL
CHAMBER 22' X 15-6 = 341 SQ.FT.
DEPTH OF CELLAR FLOOR BELOW FOOTINGS
AS ALREADY FIGVRED 3-0 GIVING 1023 CV. FT.
BACK PORCH AND FRONT STEPS 235 . .
CV. FT. IN HOVSE AND VERANDA 18711 .. ..
TOTAL CVBAGE   19969
COST PER CV. FOOT $.15
                          $2995.35
MARGIN   4.65
TOTAL COST $3000.00

DETAIL AT CORNER CHAMBER
SCALE   4 FEET

SECTION AT CENTER CHAMBER
CELLAR & AREA WALLS

DEVICE

FLOOR PLAN
SCALE   16 FEET

SERVICE YARD

COMPETITION FOR A SMALL HOVSE
OF THE BVNGALOW TYPE

DESIGN BY WALTER B. ANDERSON
25 E. 26th Street, New York, N. Y.

41

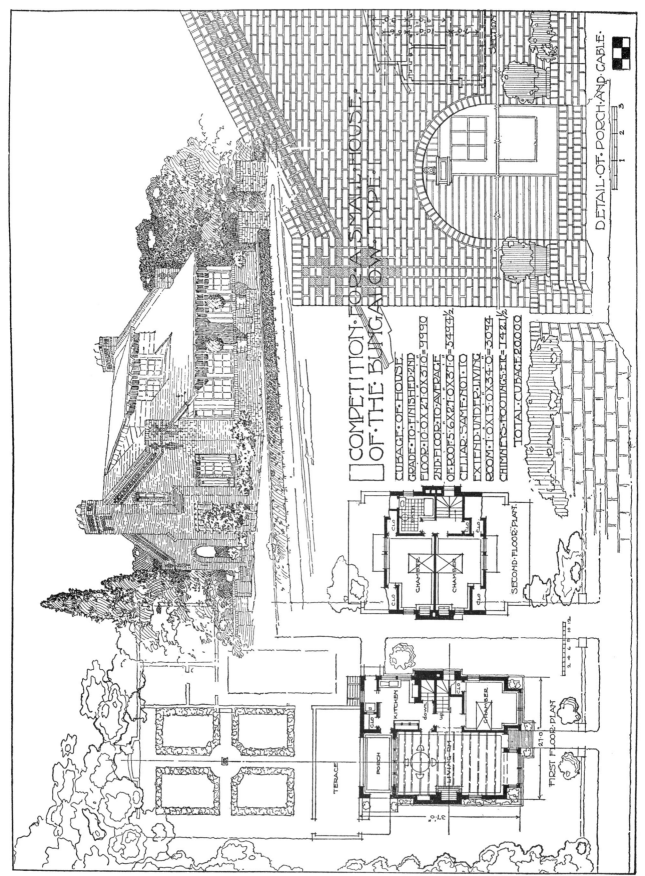

COMPETITION·FOR·A·SMALL·HOUSE·
OF·THE·BUNGALOW·TYPE·

CUBAGE·OF·HOUSE·
GRADE·TO·FINISHED·2ND
FLOOR·21'0"X27'0"X31'0" = 9990
2ND·FLOOR·TO·AVERAGE
OF·ROOF·5'6"X27'0"X31'0" = 5494½
CELLAR·SAME·NOT·10
EXTEND·UNDER·LIVING
ROOM·7'0"X15'0"X34'0" = 3094
CHIMNEYS·FOOTINGS·ETC· = 1421½
TOTAL·CUBAGE 20000·0

SECOND·FLOOR·PLAN·

FIRST·FLOOR·PLAN·

DETAIL·OF·PORCH·AND·GABLE·

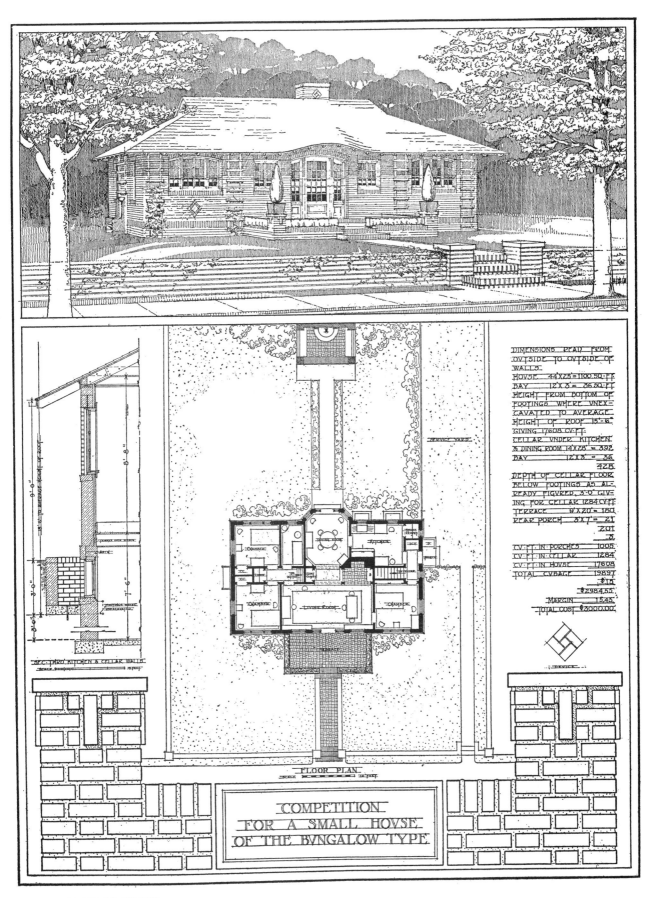

COMPETITION
FOR A SMALL HOUSE
OF THE BUNGALOW TYPE

DESIGN BY THOMAS B. TEMPLE
310 Union Avenue, Mt. Vernon, N. Y.

43

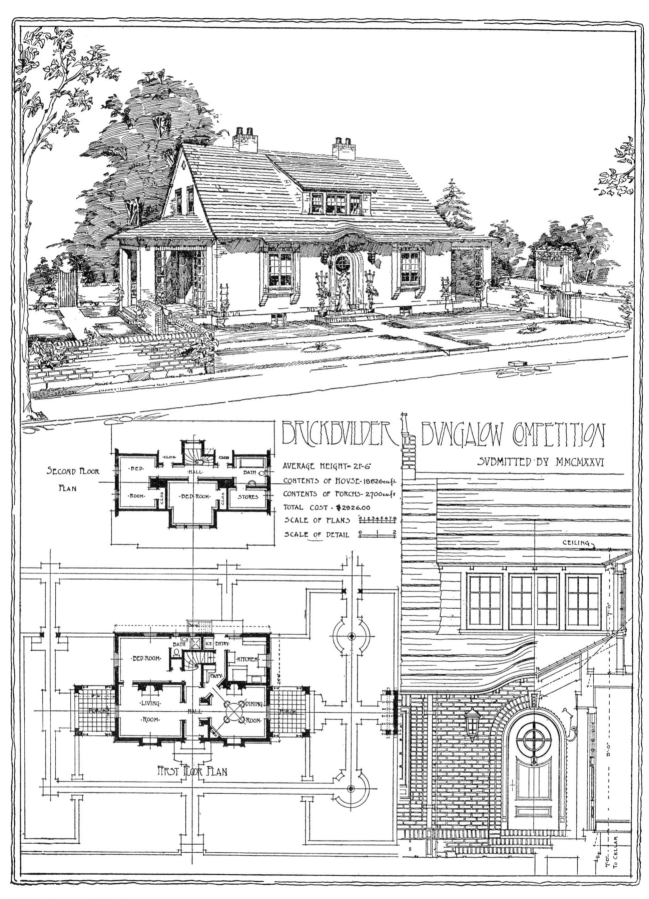

BRICKBVILDER BVNGALOW COMPETITION
SVBMITTED BY MMCMXXVI

SECOND FLOOR
PLAN

AVERAGE HEIGHT - 21'-6"
CONTENTS OF HOVSE - 18826cu.ft.
CONTENTS OF PORCHS - 2700cu.ft.
TOTAL COST - $2926.00
SCALE OF PLANS
SCALE OF DETAIL

BED.
ROOM
CLOS.
HALL
CLOS.
BATH
BED-ROOM
CLOS.
STORES

CEILING

BED-ROOM
BATH
ICE ENTRY
KITCHEN
PAN'Y
PORCH
LIVING
ROOM
HALL
DINING
ROOM
PORCH

FIRST FLOOR PLAN

TO CELLAR

DESIGN BY G. R. HOWARD GILMOUR
2415 Guilford Avenue, Baltimore, Md.

44

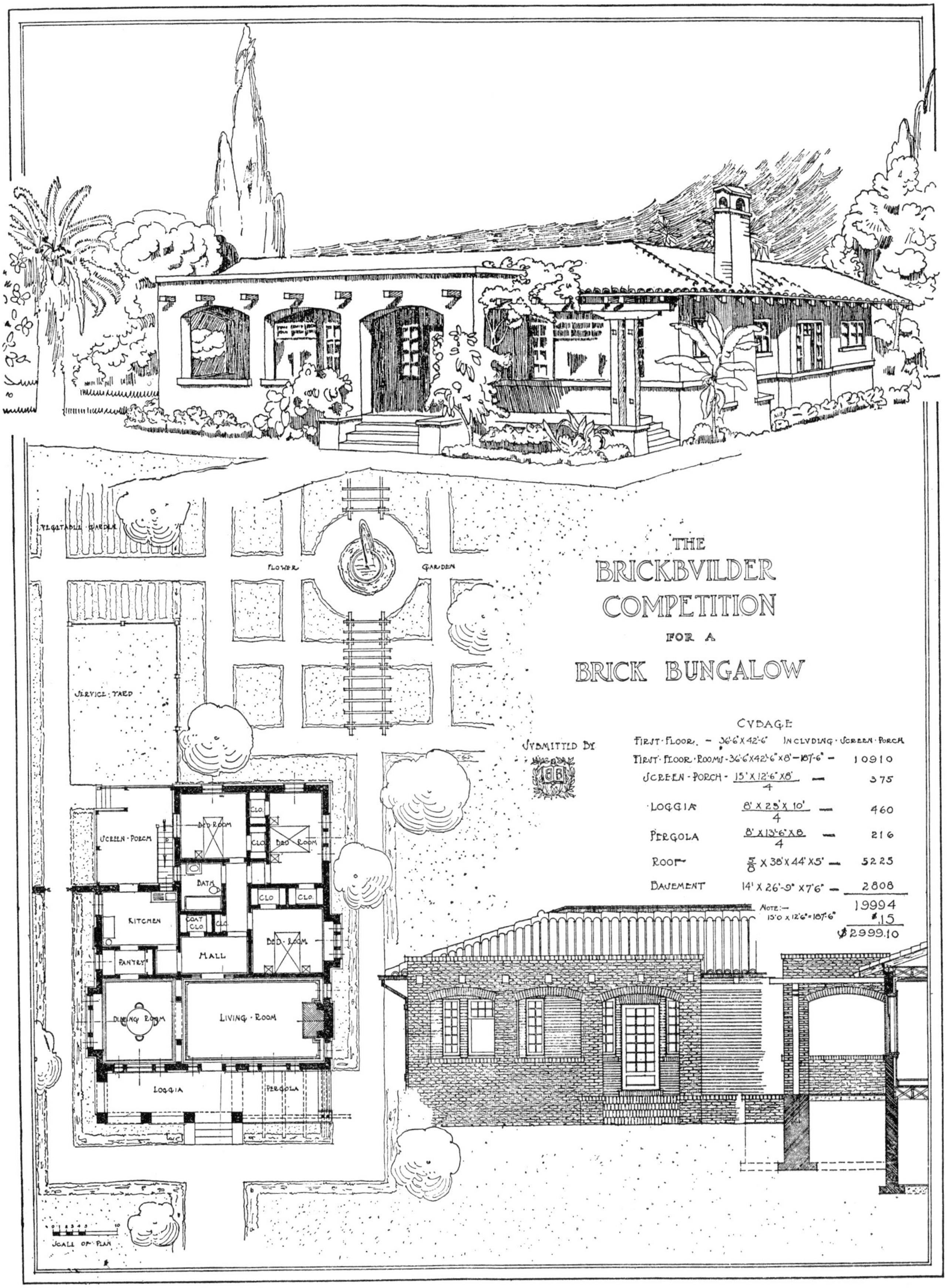
THE
BRICKBVILDER
COMPETITION
FOR A
BRICK BUNGALOW
SVBMITTED BY
CVBAGE
FIRST · FLOOR. – 36'-6" X 42'-6" INCLVDING · SCREEN · PORCH
FIRST · FLOOR · ROOMS - 36'-6" X 42'-6" X 8' – 187'-6" – 10910
SCREEN - PORCH - 15' X 12'-6" X 8' / 4 – 375
LOGGIA 8' X 23' X 10' / 4 – 460
PERGOLA 8' X 13'-6" X 8 / 4 – 216
ROOF 5/8 X 38' X 44' X 5' – 5225
BASEMENT 14' X 26'-9" X 7'6" – 2808
19994
$.15
$2999.10
NOTE:– 15'0 X 12'6" = 187'-6"
FLOWER GARDEN
SERVICE · YARD
SCREEN · PORCH
BED · ROOM
CLO
BATH
KITCHEN
COAT CLO.
PANTRY
HALL
BED · ROOM
DINING · ROOM
LIVING · ROOM
LOGGIA
PERGOLA
SCALE OF PLAN

DESIGN BY HARRY F. C. MENNECKE
412 East 15th Street, New York, N. Y.

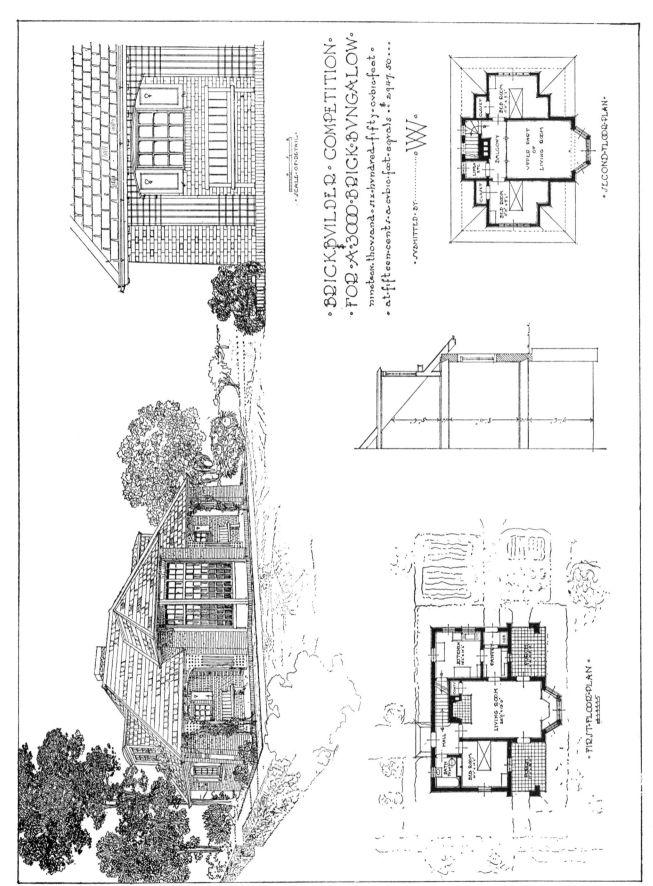

· BRICKBVILDER · COMPETITION ·
· FOR · A · 3000 · BRICK · BVNGALOW ·

nineteen · thousand · six · hundred · fifty · cubic · feet ·
· at · fifteen · cents · a · cubic · foot · equals · $ · 2947.50 · · · ·

· SVBMITTED · BY · · · · · · · · · · W ·

· SECOND · FLOOR · PLAN ·

· SCALE · OF · DETAIL ·

· FIRST · FLOOR · PLAN ·

DESIGN BY WILLIAM E. VOSS
Room 78, 8 Beacon Street, Boston, Mass.

46

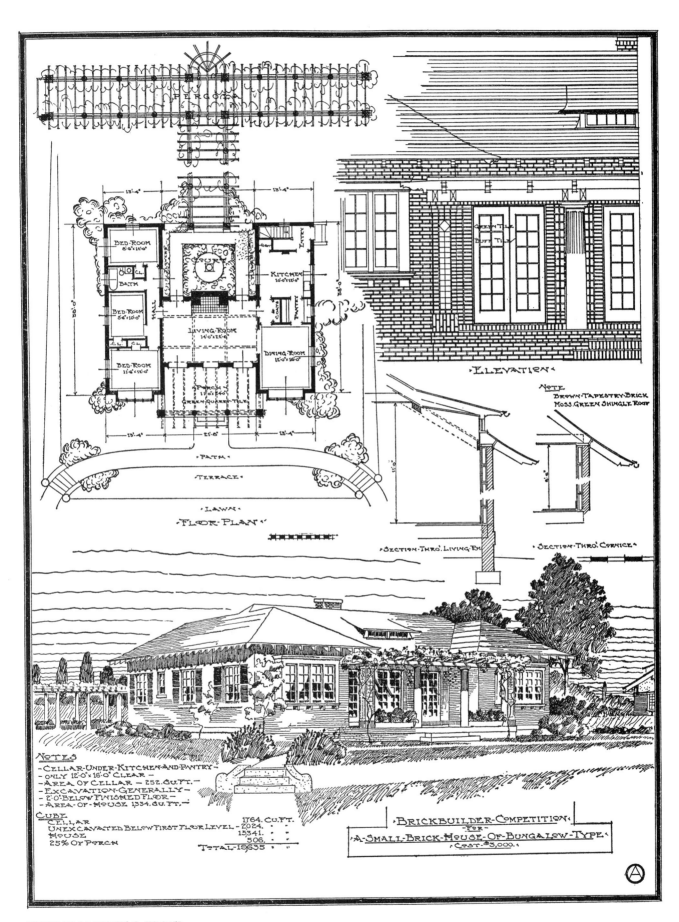

·FLOOR·PLAN·

·ELEVATION·

NOTE
BROWN·TAPESTRY·BRICK
MOSS·GREEN·SHINGLE·ROOF

·SECTION·THRO·LIVING·RM· ·SECTION·THRO·CORNICE·

NOTES
-CELLAR·UNDER·KITCHEN·AND·PANTRY-
- ONLY·12'·0"·X·16'·0"·CLEAR -
- AREA·OF·CELLAR - 252·CU·FT.-
- EXCAVATION·GENERALLY -
- 2'·0"·BELOW·FINISHED·FLOOR -
- AREA·OF·HOUSE·1534·CU·FT.-

CUBE
CELLAR   1764·CU·FT.
UNEXCAVATED·BELOW·FIRST·FLOOR·LEVEL - 2024·"·"
HOUSE   15341·"·"
25%·OF·PORCH   506·"·"
                        ·TOTAL·19635·"·"

·BRICKBUILDER·COMPETITION·
·FOR·
·A·SMALL·BRICK·HOUSE·OF·BUNGALOW·TYPE·
·COST·$5,000.·

DESIGN BY LA POINTE & SUMNER
989 Southern Boulevard, New York, N. Y.
47

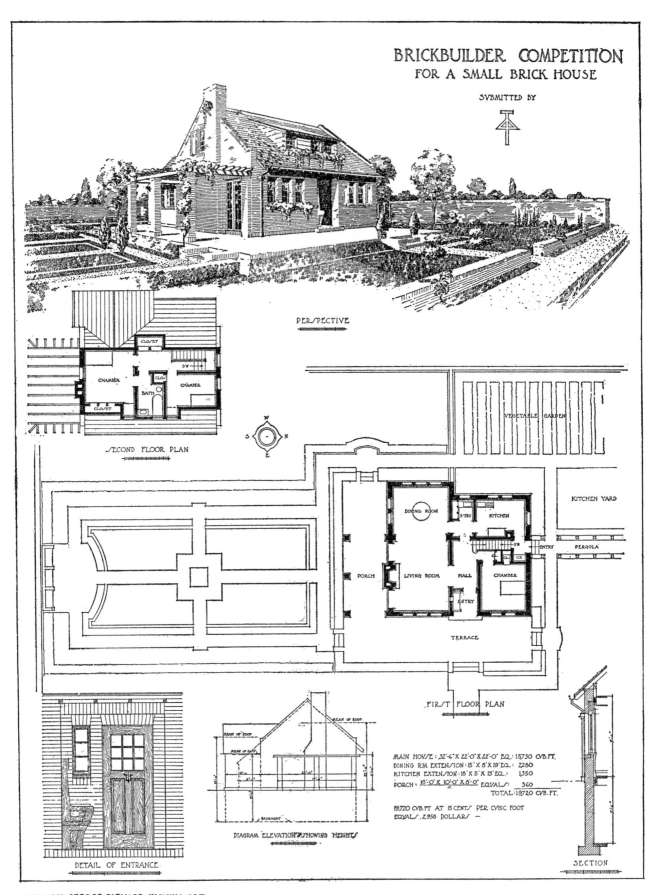

BRICKBUILDER COMPETITION
FOR A SMALL BRICK HOUSE

SVBMITTED BY

PERSPECTIVE

SECOND FLOOR PLAN

CLOSET

CHAMBER   CLOS

BATH   CHAMBER

CLOSET   D·W

VEGETABLE GARDEN

KITCHEN YARD

DINING ROOM   P'TRY   KITCHEN

PERGOLA

ENTRY

PORCH   LIVING ROOM   HALL   CHAMBER   ICE

ENTRY

TERRACE

FIRST FLOOR PLAN

DETAIL OF ENTRANCE

REAR OF ROOF.
REAR OF ROOF
REAR OF ROOF

BASEMENT

DIAGRAM ELEVATION SHOWING HEIGHTS

MAIN HOVSE : 32'-6" X 22'-0" X 22'-0" EQ.: 15730 CVB.FT.
DINING R'M EXTENSION: 15' X 8' X 19' EQ.: 2260
KITCHEN EXTENSION: 16' X 5' X 15' EQ.: 1350
PORCH : 18'-0" X 10'-0" X 6'-0" EQVALS : 360
TOTAL : 19720 CVB.FT.

19720 CVB.FT AT 15 CENTS PER CVBIC FOOT
EQVALS , 2,958 DOLLARS —

SECTION

DESIGN BY GEORGE RICHARD KLINKHARDT
672 St. Nicholas Avenue, New York, N. Y.

48

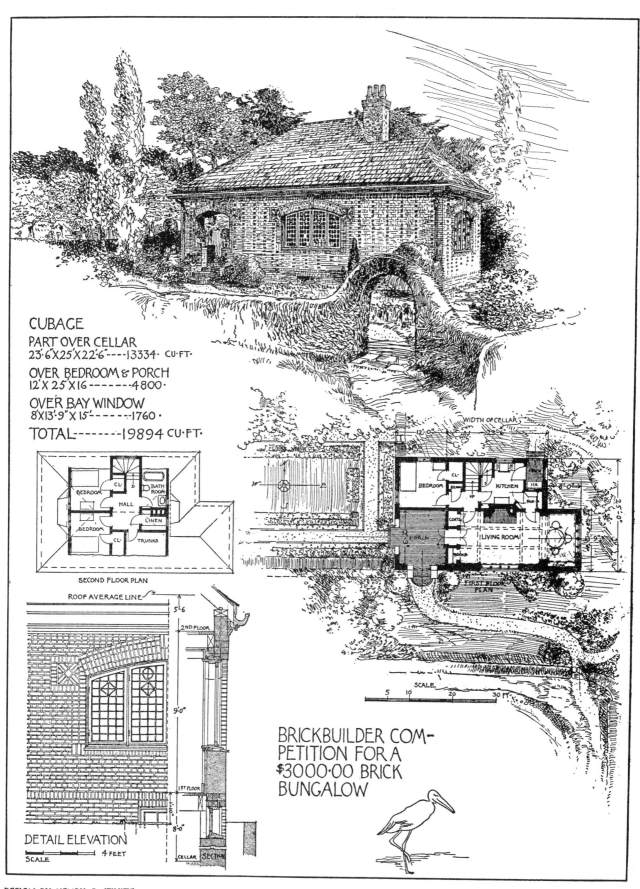

CUBAGE

PART OVER CELLAR
23'·6"X25'X22'·6"----13334· CU·FT·

OVER BEDROOM & PORCH
12'X 25'X16'------4800·

OVER BAY WINDOW
8'X13'·9"X 15'------1760·

TOTAL-------19894 CU·FT·

SECOND FLOOR PLAN

BEDROOM CL' D BATH ROOM
HALL
LINEN
BEDROOM CL' TRUNKS

WIDTH OF CELLAR

BEDROOM CL' KITCHEN
PORCH LIVING ROOM
FIRST FLOOR PLAN

ROOF AVERAGE LINE
5'·6"
2ND FLOOR
9'·0"
1ST FLOOR
8'·0"

DETAIL ELEVATION
SCALE   4 FEET

CELLAR SECTION

SCALE
5   10   20   30 FT

BRICKBUILDER COM-
PETITION FOR A
$3000·00 BRICK
BUNGALOW

DESIGN BY HENRY P. WHITE
101 Tremont Street, Boston, Mass.

49

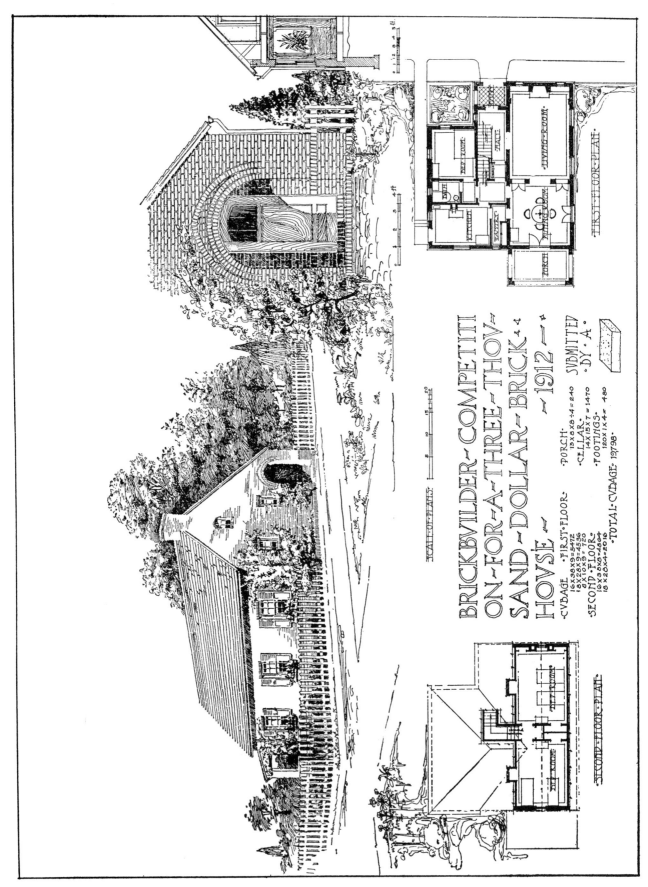

BRICKBVILDER·COMPETITI
ON·FOR·A·THREE·THOV·
SAND·DOLLAR·BRICK·
HOVSE·
~ 1912 ~

·CVBAGE· ·FIRST·FLOOR·   ·PORCH·   SVBMITTED
16x36x9=5472   12x8x8÷4=240   ·BY· A ·
18x28x9=4536   ·CELLAR·
8x10x9= 720   14x15x7=1470
·SECOND·FLOOR·   ·FOOTINGS·
16x36x8=4604   120x1x4= 480
18 x26x4=2016
        ·TOTAL·CVBAGE· 19798·

·FIRST·FLOOR·PLAN·

·SECOND·FLOOR·PLAN·

·SCALE·OF·PLANS·

DESIGN BY WILLIAM F. BURKHART, JR.
250 W. 52nd Street, New York, N. Y.

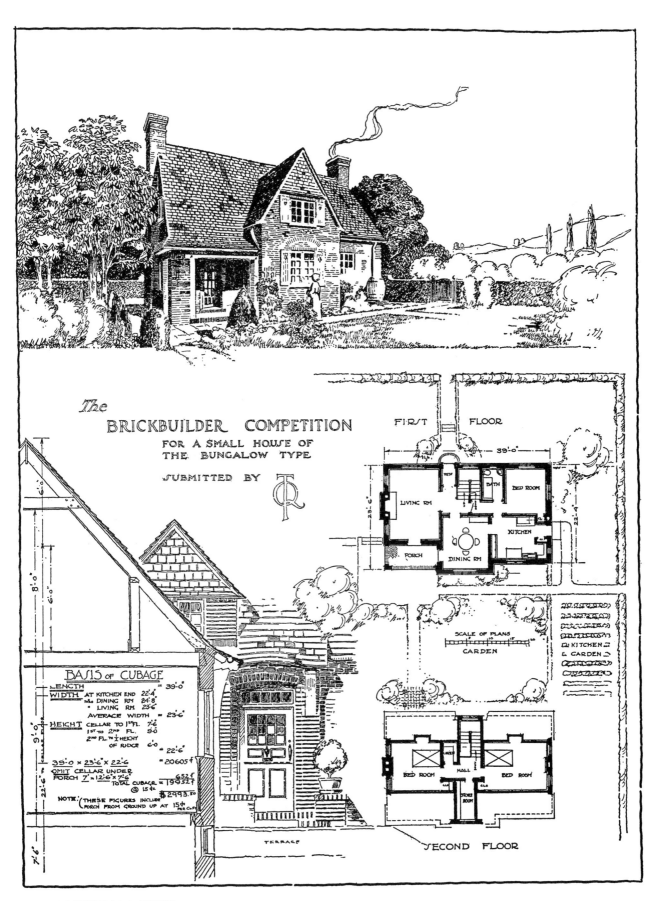

The
BRICKBUILDER COMPETITION
FOR A SMALL HOUSE OF
THE BUNGALOW TYPE

SUBMITTED BY

FIRST FLOOR

LIVING RM
BATH
BED ROOM
KITCHEN
PORCH
DINING RM

SCALE OF PLANS
GARDEN

KITCHEN & GARDEN

BED ROOM
HALL
BED ROOM
STORE ROOM

SECOND FLOOR

BASIS of CUBAGE

LENGTH = 39'-0"
WIDTH AT KITCHEN END 22'-4"
DINING RM 24'-8"
LIVING RM 23'-6"
AVERAGE WIDTH = 23'-6"
HEIGHT CELLAR TO 1ST FL. 7'-6"
1ST to 2ND FL. 9'-0"
2ND FL. ½ HEIGHT
OF RIDGE 6'-0" = 22'-6"

39'-0" × 23'-6" × 22'-6" = 20605 f
OMIT CELLAR UNDER
PORCH 7' × 12'-6" × 7'-6" 652 f
TOTAL CUBAGE = 19952 f
@ 15¢ = $2993.50
NOTE: THESE FIGURES INCLUDE
PORCH FROM GROUND UP AT 15¢ PER CU.FT.

TERRACE

DESIGN BY WETHERILL P. TROUT
328 Chestnut Street, Philadelphia, Pa.

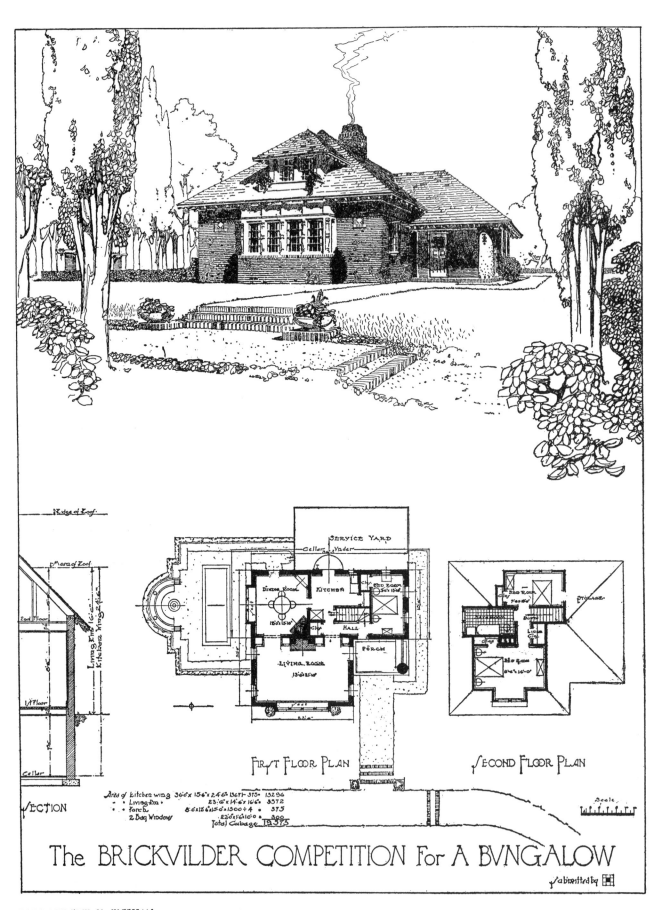

SECTION

FIRST FLOOR PLAN

SECOND FLOOR PLAN

Area of Kitchen wing 36'0" x 15'6" x 24'6" = 13671 - 375 = 13296
" " Living Rm " 23'-6" x 14'-6" x 16'6" = 8372
" " Porch 8'-6" x 16'-6" x 15'-0" = 1300 ÷ 4 = 375
2 Bay Windows 22'-6" x 16'-0"-0" = 300
Total Cubage 19375

The BRICKVILDER COMPETITION For A BVNGALOW

submitted by

DESIGN BY EMIL H. KLEEMAN
741 Broad Street, Newark, N. J.

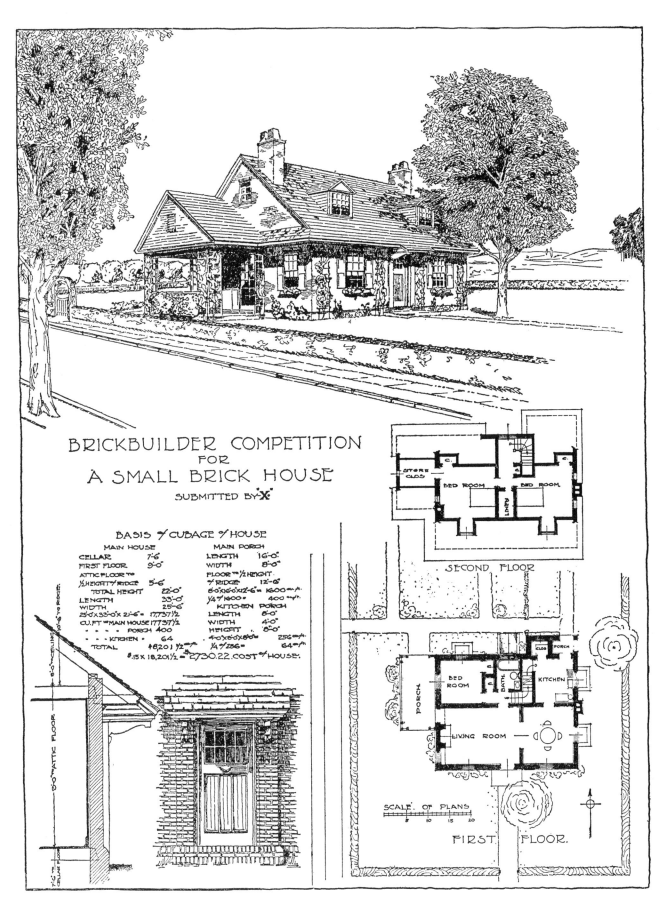

BRICKBUILDER COMPETITION
FOR
A SMALL BRICK HOUSE
SUBMITTED BY "X"

BASIS of CUBAGE of HOUSE

MAIN HOUSE

CELLAR	7'-6"
FIRST FLOOR	9'-0"
ATTIC FLOOR to	
½ HEIGHT of RIDGE	5'-6"
TOTAL HEIGHT	22'-0"
LENGTH	33'-0"
WIDTH	25'-6"
25'-0"X 33'-0"X 21'-6" =	17,737½
CU.FT to MAIN HOUSE	17737½
" " " PORCH	400
" " " KITCHEN	64
TOTAL	18,201½

MAIN PORCH

LENGTH	16'-0"
WIDTH	8'-0"
FLOOR to ½ HEIGHT	
of RIDGE	12'-6"
8'-0"X16'-0"X12'-6" =	1600 cu. ft.
¼ of 1600 =	400 cu. ft.

KITCHEN PORCH

LENGTH	8'-0"
WIDTH	4'-0"
HEIGHT	8'-0"
4'-0"X8'-0"X8'-0" =	256 cu. ft.
¼ of 256 =	64 cu. ft.

#.15 X 18,201½ = 2730.22. COST of HOUSE.

SECOND FLOOR

STORE CLOS. | C. | C.
BED ROOM | HALL | BED ROOM

FIRST FLOOR.

PORCH | BED ROOM | BATH | KITCHEN | CLOS | PORCH
LIVING ROOM

SCALE of PLANS
5 10 15 20

DESIGN BY WALLACE M. BAXTER
328 Chestnut Street, Philadelphia, Pa.

53

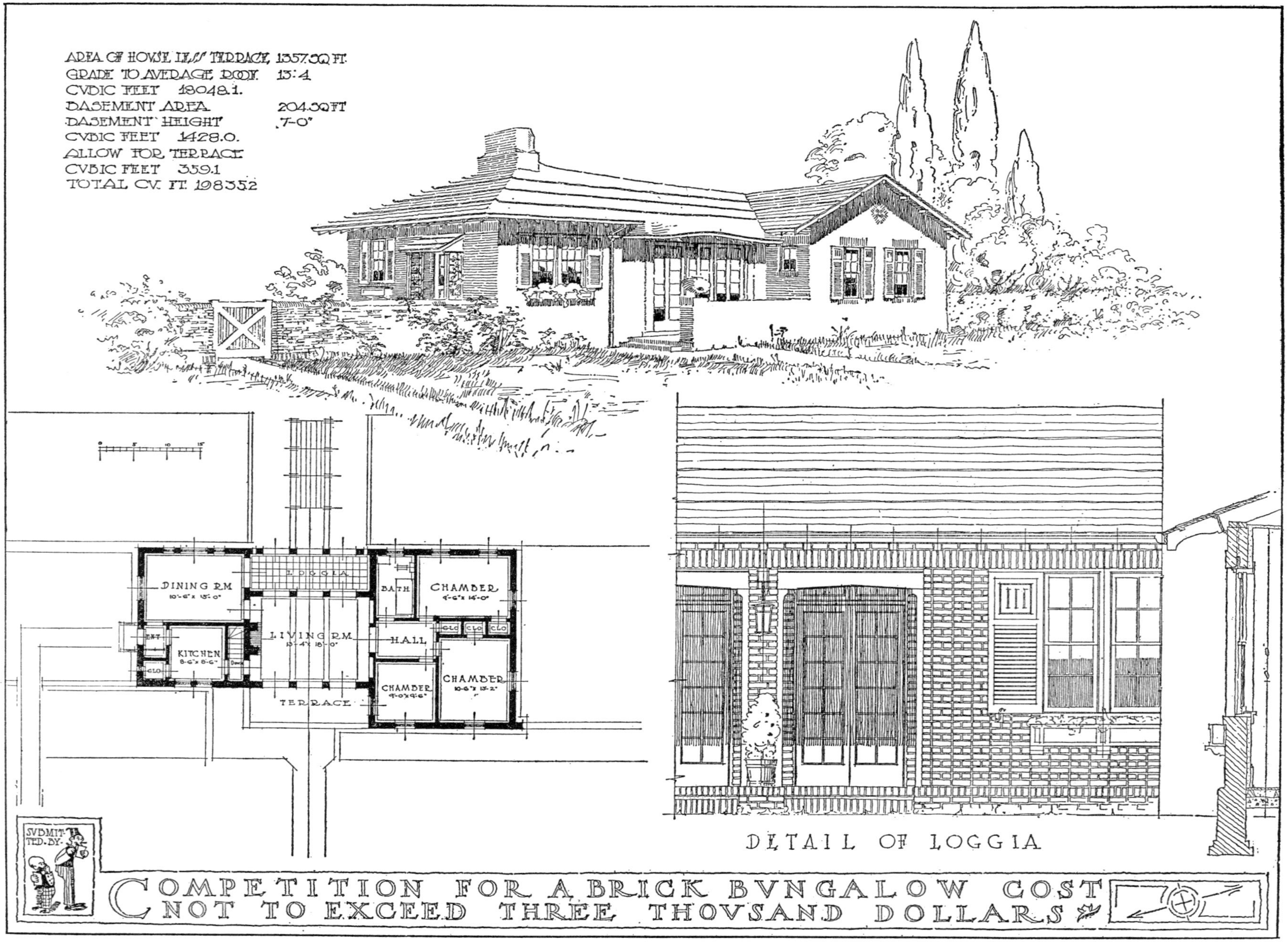
AREA OF HOUSE LESS TERRACE, 1357 SQ FT
GRADE TO AVERAGE ROOF 13'-4
CUBIC FEET 18048.1.
BASEMENT AREA 204 SQ FT
BASEMENT HEIGHT 7'-0"
CUBIC FEET 1428.0.
ALLOW FOR TERRACE
CUBIC FEET 359.1
TOTAL CU. FT. 19835.2
DINING RM 10'-6" x 15'-0"
KITCHEN 8'-6" x 8'-6"
LOGGIA
LIVING RM 13'-4" x 18'-0"
TERRACE
BATH
HALL
CHAMBER 9'-6" x 14'-0"
CHAMBER 10'-6" x 13'-2"
CHAMBER 9'-0" x 9'-6"
CLO
DETAIL OF LOGGIA
SUBMITTED BY
COMPETITION FOR A BRICK BUNGALOW COST NOT TO EXCEED THREE THOUSAND DOLLARS

DESIGN BY LOUIS R. MOSS & ROBERT C. LEHMAN
500 Seaboard Bank Building, Norfolk, Va.

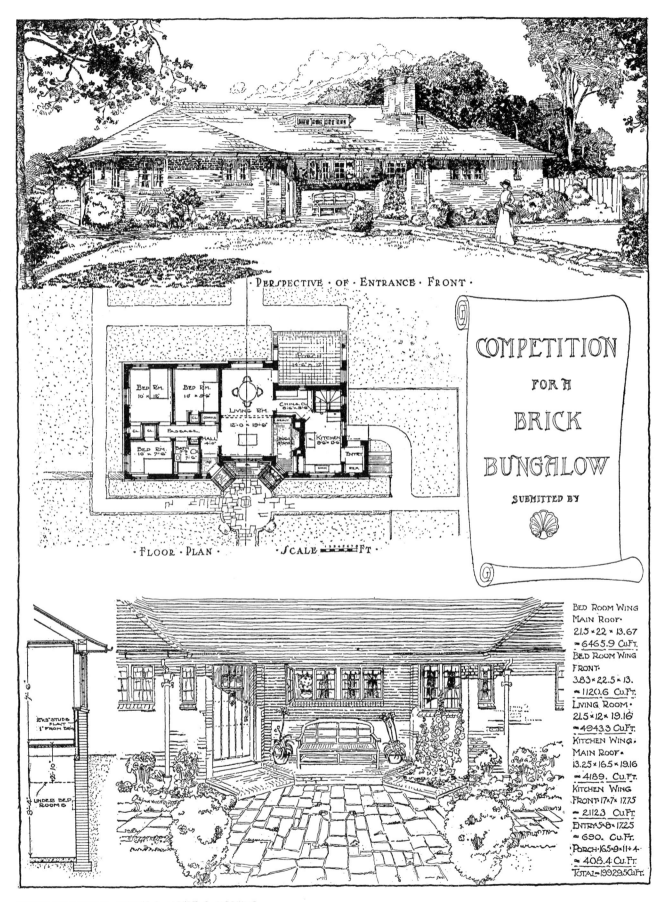

· PERSPECTIVE · OF · ENTRANCE · FRONT ·

BED RM.
10 × 12
BED RM.
10 × 9-6
PORCH
14-6 × 12
LIVING RM
12-0 × 19-6
CHINA CL
8-6 × 5-9
KITCHEN
8-6 × 13-6
PASSAGE
HALL
4-0
BED RM.
10 × 7-6
BATH
5-9
7-6
ENTRY

COMPETITION

FOR A

BRICK

BUNGALOW

SUBMITTED BY

· FLOOR · PLAN ·   · SCALE —— FT ·

2×3 STUDS
FLAT
1" FROM DEN
7-6
2-5-10
8-0
UNDER BED
ROOMS

BED ROOM WING
MAIN ROOF ·
21.5 × 22 × 13.67
= 6465.9 CU.FT.
BED ROOM WING
FRONT ·
3.83 × 22.5 × 13.
= 1120.6 CU.FT.
LIVING ROOM ·
21.5 × 12 × 19.16
= 4943.3 CU.FT.
KITCHEN WING ·
MAIN ROOF ·
13.25 × 16.5 × 19.16
= 4189. CU.FT.
KITCHEN WING
FRONT 17 × 7 × 17.75
= 2112.3 CU.FT.
ENTRY 5 × 8 × 17.25
= 690. CU.FT.
PORCH · 16.5 × 9 × 11 ÷ 4 ·
= 408.4 CU.FT.
TOTAL = 19929.5 CU.FT.

DESIGN BY DAVID D. BARNES & ALBERT G. HOPKINS
15 Beacon Street, Boston, Mass.

55

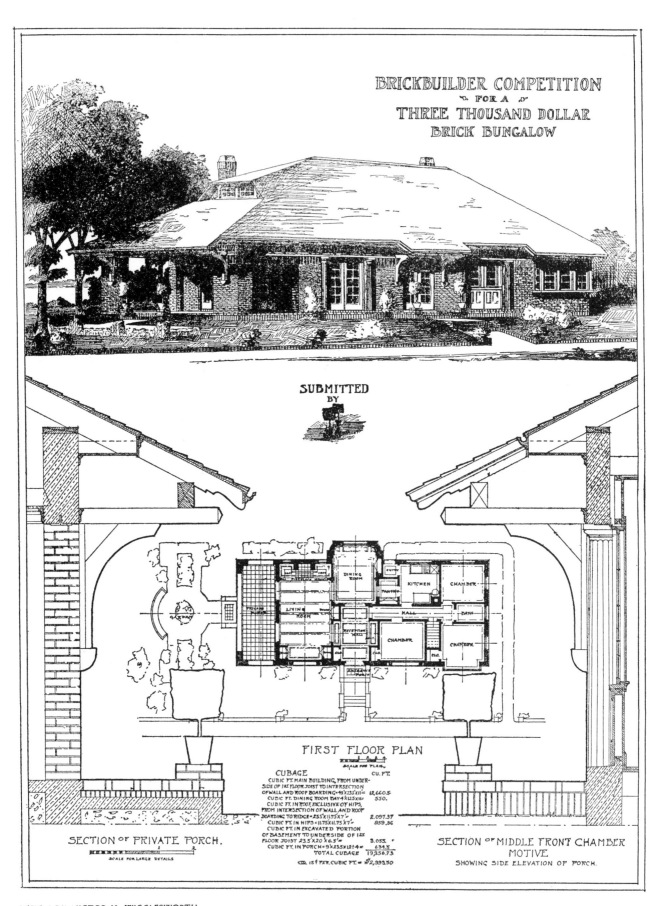

BRICKBUILDER COMPETITION
FOR A
THREE THOUSAND DOLLAR
BRICK BUNGALOW

SUBMITTED
BY

FIRST FLOOR PLAN

SCALE FOR PLAN

CUBAGE   CU. FT.
CUBIC FT. MAIN BUILDING, FROM UNDER-
SIDE OF 1ST FLOOR JOIST TO INTERSECTION
OF WALL AND ROOF BOARDING=49X235XII=   12,660.5
CUBIC FT. DINING ROOM BAY 4X125XII=   550.
CUBIC FT. IN ROOF, EXCLUSIVE OF HIPS,
FROM INTERSECTION OF WALL AND ROOF
BOARDING TO RIDGE=235XII.75X7'=   2,097.37
CUBIC FT. IN HIPS=II.75XII.75X7'=   959.86
CUBIC FT. IN EXCAVATED PORTION
OF BASEMENT TO UNDERSIDE OF 1ST
FLOOR JOIST 23.5'X20'X6.5'=   3,055.
CUBIC FT. IN PORCH=9X235XI2÷4=   634.5
            TOTAL CUBAGE   19,956.73
       @ 15¢ PER CUBIC FT. = $2,993.50

SECTION OF PRIVATE PORCH.

SCALE FOR LARGE DETAILS

SECTION OF MIDDLE FRONT CHAMBER
MOTIVE
SHOWING SIDE ELEVATION OF PORCH.

DESIGN BY VICTOR H. WIGGLESWORTH
320 Boylston Street, Boston, Mass.

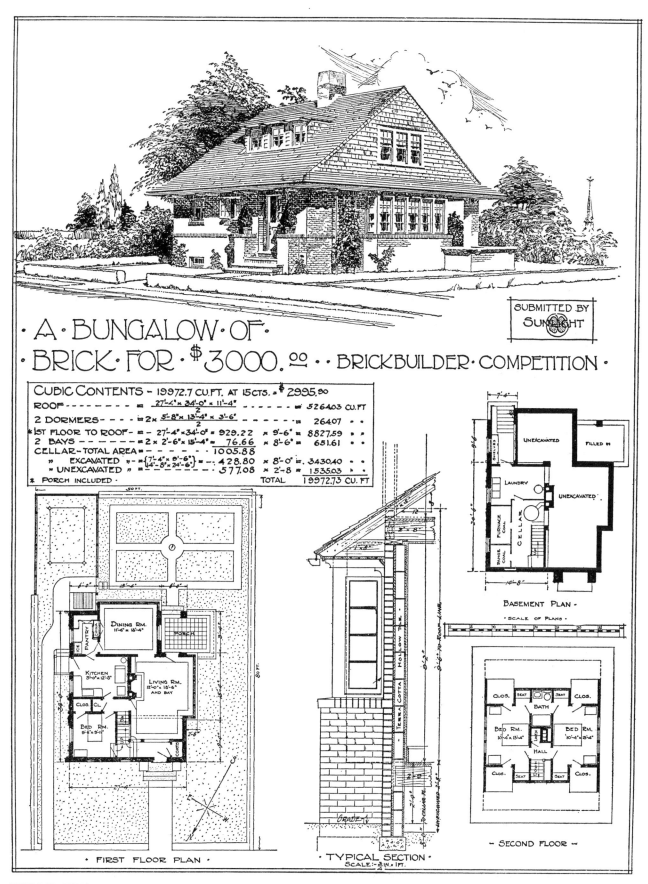

· A · BUNGALOW · OF · · BRICK · FOR · $3000.⁰⁰ · · BRICKBUILDER · COMPETITION ·

SUBMITTED BY
SUNLIGHT

CUBIC CONTENTS - 19972.7 CU. FT. AT 15 CTS. = $2995.90

ROOF	= 27'-4" × 34'-0" × 11'-4" / 2	=	5264.03 CU. FT
2 DORMERS	= 2 × 5'-8" × 13'-4" × 3'-6" / 2	=	264.07
*1ST FLOOR TO ROOF	= 27'-4" × 34'-0" = 929.22 × 9'-6"	=	8827.59
2 BAYS	= 2 × 2'-6" × 15'-4" = 76.66 × 8'-6"	=	651.61
CELLAR - TOTAL AREA	= 1005.88		
" EXCAVATED	= {7'-4" × 9'-6"} = 428.80 × 8'-0" = {4'-8" × 24'-6"}		3430.40
" UNEXCAVATED	= 577.08 × 2'-8		1535.03
* PORCH INCLUDED ·		TOTAL	19972.73 CU. FT.

BASEMENT PLAN ·

· SCALE OF PLANS ·

- SECOND FLOOR -

· FIRST FLOOR PLAN ·

· TYPICAL SECTION ·
SCALE :- ¾ IN. 1 FT.

DESIGN BY RUSSELL H. SHAW
735 Grosvenor Building, Providence, R. I.

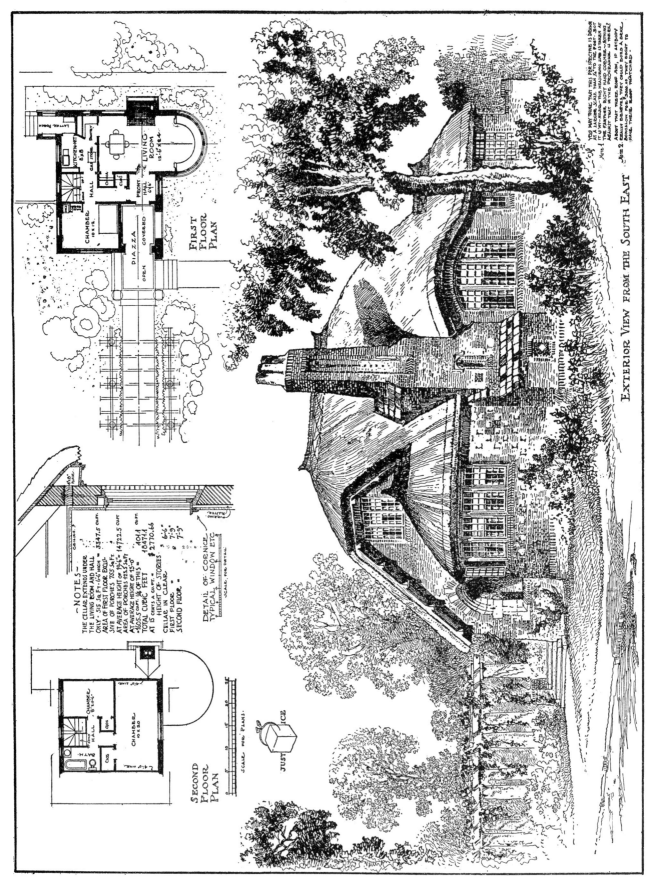

FIRST FLOOR PLAN

LIVING ROOM
13'-6"x16'4"

CHAMBER
10x12

KITCHENETTE
6x8

FRONT HALL
6x6

DIAZZA
OPEN   COVERED

SECOND FLOOR PLAN

CHAMBER
10x20

CHAMBER
8x10

HALL

BATH

—NOTES—
THE CELLAR EXTENDS UNDER
THE LIVING ROOM AND HALL
ONLY - 515 Sq. Ft.-6'-6" HIGH =   3347.5 CU.FT.
AREA OF FIRST FLOOR EXCLU-
SIVE OF PORCHES 755 Sq.Ft.
AT AVERAGE HEIGHT OF 19'6" = 14722.5 CU.FT.
AREA OF PORCHES 123.5 Sq.Ft.
AT AVERAGE HEIGHT OF 15'-0" =
1605.5 CU.FT. ¼ OF THIS =   401.4 CU.FT.
TOTAL CUBIC FEET   18471.4
AT 15 CENTS A CU.FT. = $2770.66

HEIGHT OF STORIES
CELLAR IN CLEAR   6'-6"
FIRST FLOOR   7'-9"
SECOND FLOOR   7'-9"

DETAIL OF CORNICE
TYPICAL WINDOW ETC.
SCALE FOR DETAIL

SCALE FOR PLANS

JUST ICE

EXTERIOR VIEW FROM THE SOUTH EAST

58

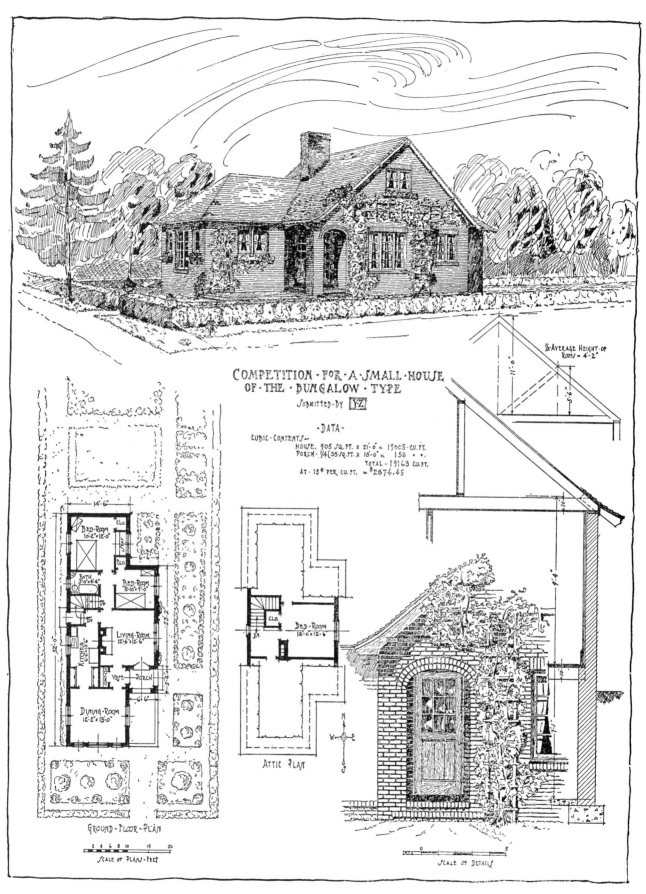

COMPETITION·FOR·A·SMALL·HOUSE
OF·THE·BUNGALOW·TYPE
SUBMITTED·BY YZ

-DATA-
CUBIC·CONTENTS:-
HOUSE· 905 SQ. FT. × 21'-0" = 19005 CU. FT.
PORCH· ¼(35 SQ. FT. × 18'-0") = 158 " "·
TOTAL· 19163 CU. FT.
AT· 15¢ PER CU. FT. = $2874.45

½ AVERAGE·HEIGHT·OF
ROOFS = 4'-2"

BED-ROOM
10'-2" × 12'-0"

BATH
5'-0" × 6'-6"

BED-ROOM
8'-10" × 9'-0"

LIVING-ROOM
12'-6" × 12'-6"

KITCHEN

VEST.

PORCH

DINING-ROOM
12'-2" × 15'-0"

GROUND·FLOOR·PLAN

2 4 6 8 10   15   20
SCALE OF PLANS-FEET

BED-ROOM
12'-0" × 12'-6"

ATTIC PLAN

N
W   E
S

0   5
SCALE OF DETAILS

DESIGN BY ERNEST C. WEISSBACH
217 East 18th Street, New York, N. Y.

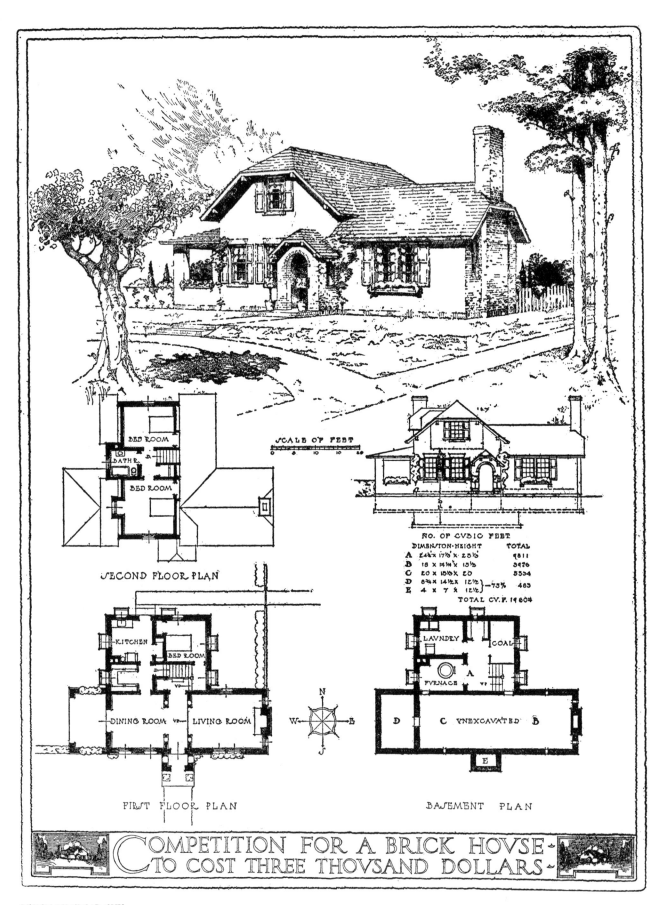

SCALE OF FEET

SECOND FLOOR PLAN

NO. OF CUBIC FEET

	DIMENSION · HEIGHT	TOTAL
A	24½' x 17⅓' x 25½'	9811
B	18 x 14¼ x 13½	3476
C	20 x 13⅝ x 20	5534
D	8¾ x 14½ x 12½ }—75%	483
E	4 x 7½ x 12½	

TOTAL CV.F. 19 804

KITCHEN   BED ROOM

DINING ROOM   LIVING ROOM

LAUNDRY   COAL

FURNACE   A

D   C UNEXCAVATED   B

E

N
W   E
S

FIRST FLOOR PLAN   BASEMENT PLAN

COMPETITION FOR A BRICK HOUSE
TO COST THREE THOUSAND DOLLARS

DESIGN BY EDGAR GUY
201 Lee Avenue, Toronto, Ont , Can.

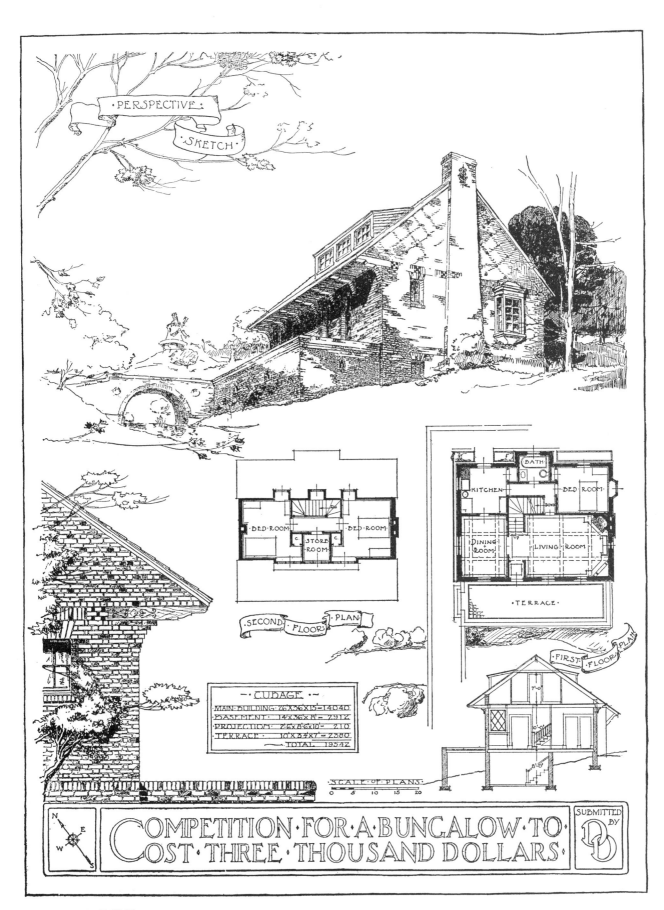

·PERSPECTIVE·
·SKETCH·

·SECOND· FLOOR· PLAN·

BED·ROOM   BED·ROOM
STORE·ROOM

BATH
KITCHEN   BED·ROOM
DINING·ROOM   LIVING·ROOM
·TERRACE·

·FIRST· FLOOR· PLAN·

~·CUBAGE·~
MAIN·BUILDING·26'X36'X15'=14040
BASEMENT· 14'X36'X8'= 7912
PROJECTION· 2'6X8'6X10'= 210
TERRACE· 10'X34'X7'= 2380
TOTAL· 19542

SCALE·OF·PLANS
0   5   10   15   20

N
E
W
S

·COMPETITION·FOR·A·BUNGALOW·TO·
·COST·THREE·THOUSAND·DOLLARS·

SUBMITTED BY
DB

DESIGN BY J. H. TAYLOR
12 Beaver Hall Square, Montreal, Que., Can.

61

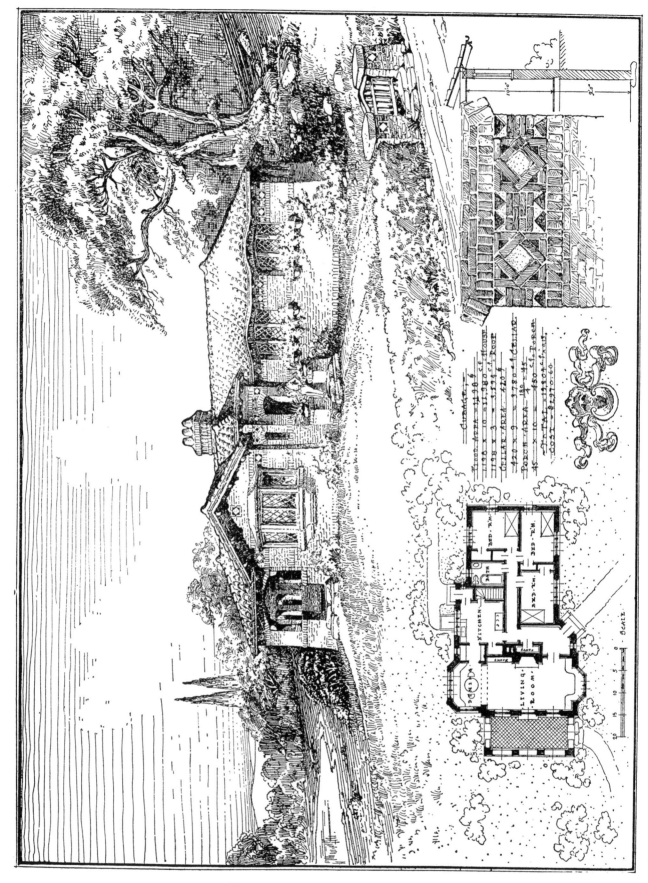

DESIGN BY HAROLD FIELD KELLOGG
20 Beacon Street, Boston, Mass.

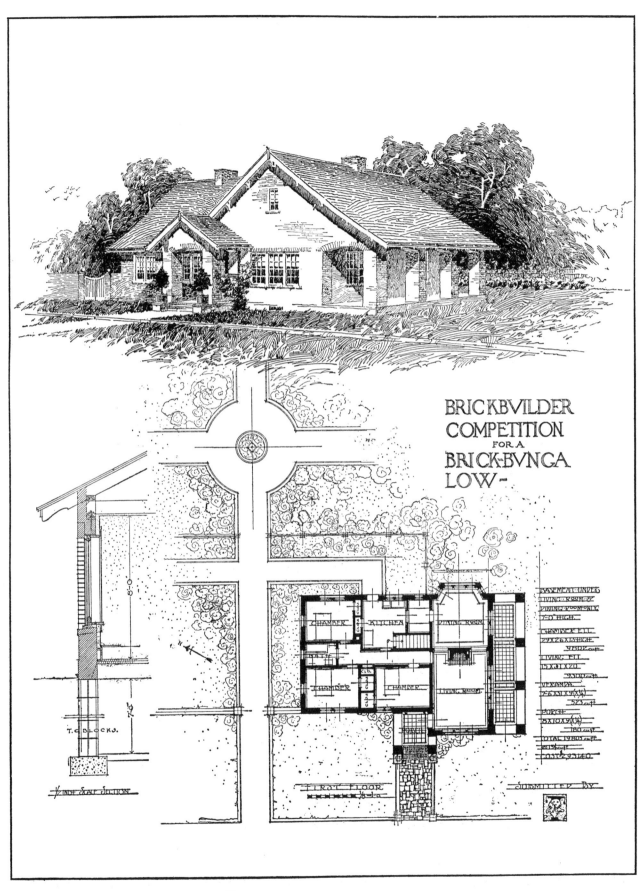

BRICKBVILDER
COMPETITION
FOR A
BRICK·BVNGA
LOW·

DESIGN BY PHILIP S. AVERY & LLOYD A. PATRICK
4 Boyleston Terrace, W. Medford, Mass.

63

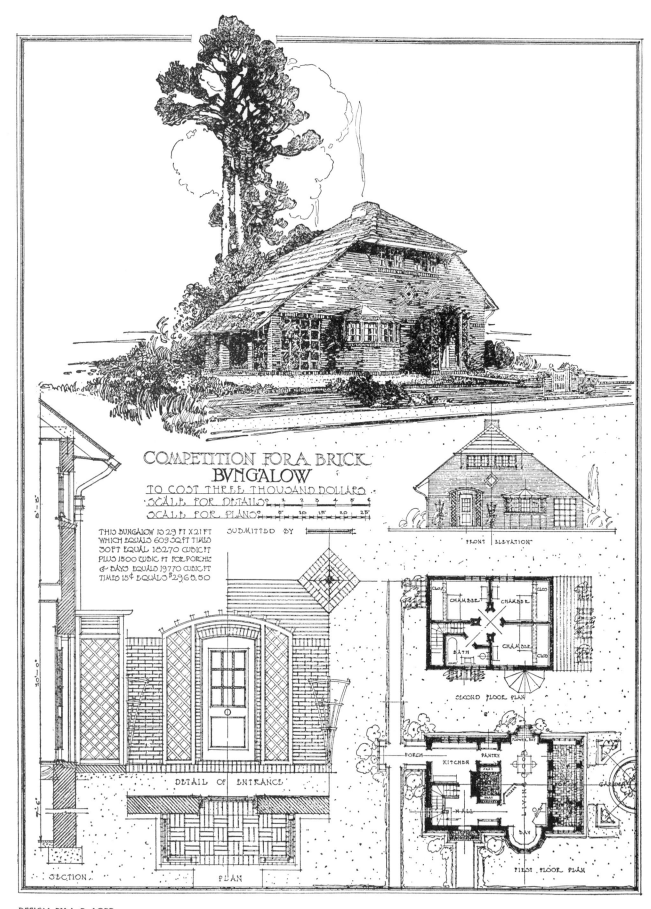

COMPETITION FOR A BRICK
BVNGALOW
TO COST THREE THOUSAND DOLLARS
SCALE FOR DETAILS
SCALE FOR PLANS

THIS BUNGALOW IS 29 FT X 21 FT
WHICH EQUALS 609 SQ FT TIMES
30 FT EQUAL 18270 CUBIC FT
PLUS 1500 CUBIC FT FOR PORCHES
& BAYS EQUALS 19770 CUBIC FT
TIMES 15¢ EQUALS $2965.50

SUBMITTED BY

FRONT ELEVATION

DETAIL OF ENTRANCE

SECTION

PLAN

SECOND FLOOR PLAN

FIRST FLOOR PLAN

DESIGN BY I. P. LORD
31 Beacon Street, Boston, Mass.

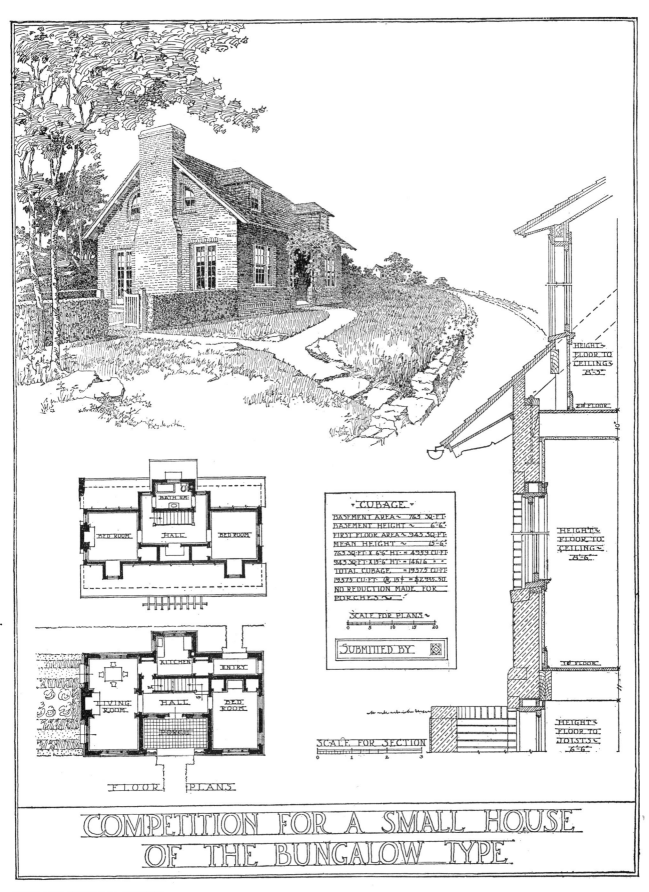

· CUBAGE ·

BASEMENT AREA ~ 763 SQ·FT·
BASEMENT HEIGHT ~ 6'-6"·
FIRST FLOOR AREA ~ 943 SQ·FT·
MEAN HEIGHT ~ 15'-6"·
763 SQ·FT· X 6'-6" HT· = 4959 CU·FT·
943 SQ·FT· X 15'-6" HT· = 14616 " "
TOTAL CUBAGE = 19575 CU·FT·
19575 CU·FT· @ 15¢ = $2,936.30
NO REDUCTION MADE FOR
PORCHES ~

SCALE FOR PLANS ~

SUBMITTED BY

HEIGHT·
FLOOR·TO
CEILINGS
8'-5"

2ND FLOOR

HEIGHT·
FLOOR·TO
CEILING ~
8'-6"

1ST·FLOOR

HEIGHT·
FLOOR·TO
JOISTS ~
6'-6"

BATH·RM·

HALL

BED·ROOM

BED·ROOM

KITCHEN

ENTRY

LIVING
ROOM

HALL

BED
ROOM

PORCH

SCALE FOR SECTION

FLOOR PLANS

COMPETITION FOR A SMALL HOUSE
OF THE BUNGALOW TYPE

DESIGN BY CHARLES T. INGHAM
323 Fourth Avenue, Pittsburgh, Pa.

65

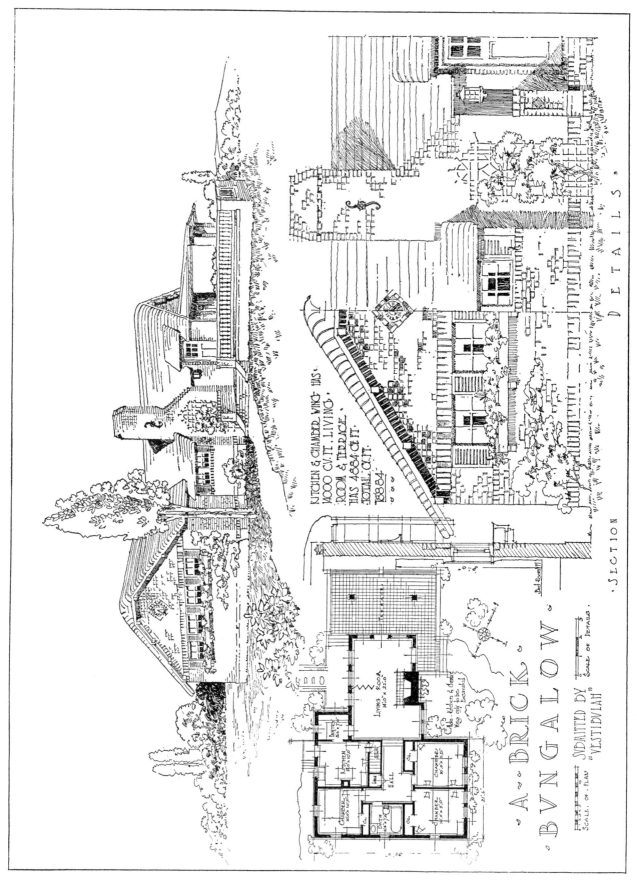

·A· BRICK·
·BVNGALOW·

SVBMITTED BY
"VESTIBVLAH"

SCALE OF PLAN

DETAILS

SECTION

KITCHEN & CHAMBER WING· HAS·
14000 CV.FT. LIVING·
ROOM & TERRACE·
HAS 4884 CV.FT·
TOTAL CV.FT·
18884

LIVING ROOM
14·0" x 21·0

HALL

KITCHEN
10·0" x 10·0

CHAMBER
16·0 x 10·0

CHAMBER
16·0 x 10·0

BATH

PANTRY

DESIGN BY GEORGE F. BLOUNT
110 State Street, Boston, Mass.

COMPETITION
FOR
A SMALL HOVSE
OF
THE BVNGALOW TYPE

≤TO BE BVILT OF BRICK COST NOT TO EXCEED 3000≥
≤TOTAL CVBAGE 19685 F≥
≤SCALE≥

CELLAR TO 2ND FLOOR LEVEL
24 X 32½ X 18 = 14040 CV FT
2ND FLOOR LEVEL TO RIDGE
24 X 32½ X 6¼ = 4875
FRONT PORCH ¼ CV FT
8 X 32½ X 2½ = 650
BACK PORCH ¼ CV FT
4 X 12 X 8½ = 180
TOTAL 19685 CV

DESIGN BY CARRINGTON FOSTER
806 17th Street, N. W., Washington, D. C.

67

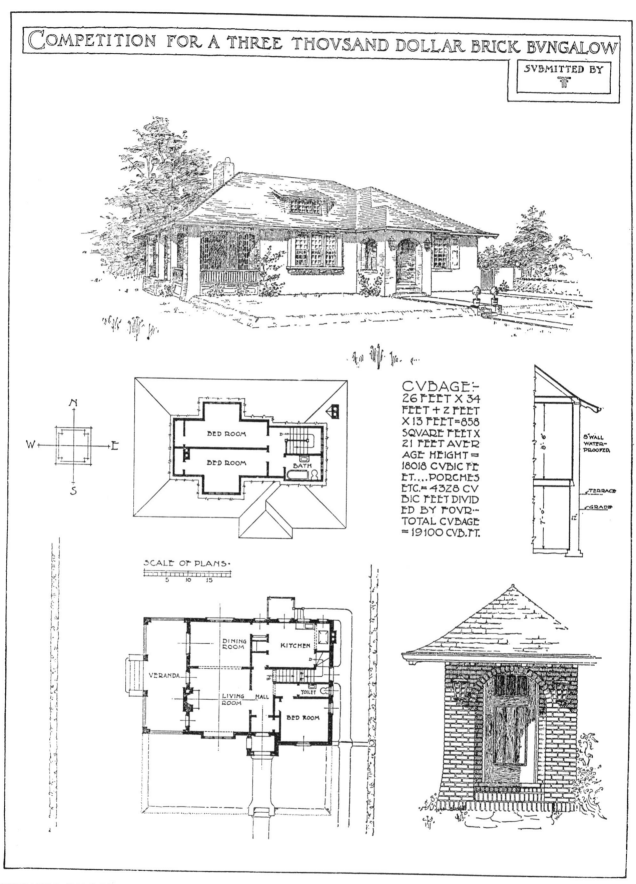

SVBMITTED BY

N
W — E
S

BED ROOM

BED ROOM

BATH

CVBAGE:-
26 FEET X 34
FEET + 2 FEET
X 13 FEET = 858
SQVARE FEET X
21 FEET AVER
AGE HEIGHT =
18018 CVBIC FE
ET....PORCHES
ETC. = 4328 CV
BIC FEET DIVID
ED BY FOVR:-
TOTAL CVBAGE
= 19100 CVB.FT.

8' WALL
WATER-
PROOFED

TERRACE
GRADE

SCALE OF PLANS.

5   10   15

DINING
ROOM

KITCHEN

VERANDA

LIVING   HALL
ROOM

TOILET

BED ROOM

DESIGN BY B. FRANK KELLY
701 Bank of Hamilton Building, Hamilton, Ont., Can.

68

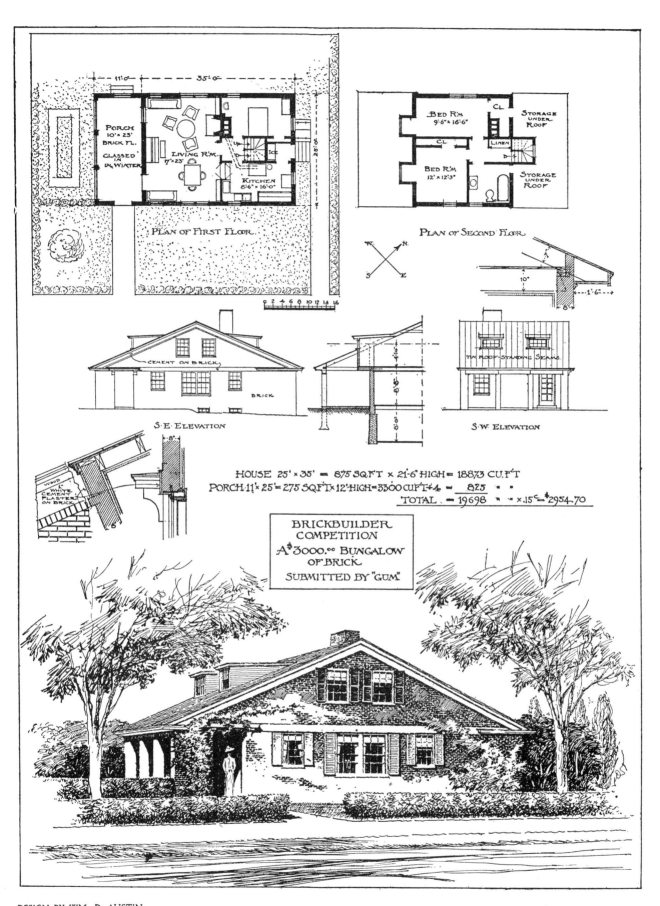

PORCH
10' x 23'
BRICK FL.

GLASSED
IN IN WINTER

LIVING R'M.
17' x 23'

KITCHEN
8'-6" x 16'-0"

PLAN OF FIRST FLOOR.

BED R'M
9'-6" x 16'-6"

CL.

CL.

LINEN

STORAGE
UNDER
ROOF

BED R'M
12' x 12'-3"

STORAGE
UNDER
ROOF

PLAN OF SECOND FLOOR

W   N

S   E

10"

1'-6"

8"

CEMENT ON BRICK

BRICK

S·E· ELEVATION

TIN ROOF·STANDING SEAMS.

S·W· ELEVATION

WOOD
WHITE
CEMENT
PLASTER
ON BRICK

8"

HOUSE 25' x 35' = 875 SQ·F'T x 21'-6" HIGH = 18873 CU·F'T
PORCH·11'x 25'= 275 SQ·F'T x 12'HIGH=3300 CU·F'T÷4 =   825   "   "
                                    TOTAL = 19698 "   " x .15ᶜ = $2954.70

BRICKBUILDER
COMPETITION
A $3000.⁰⁰ BUNGALOW
OF BRICK

SUBMITTED BY "GUM"

DESIGN BY WM. D. AUSTIN
50 Bromfield Street, Boston, Mass.

69

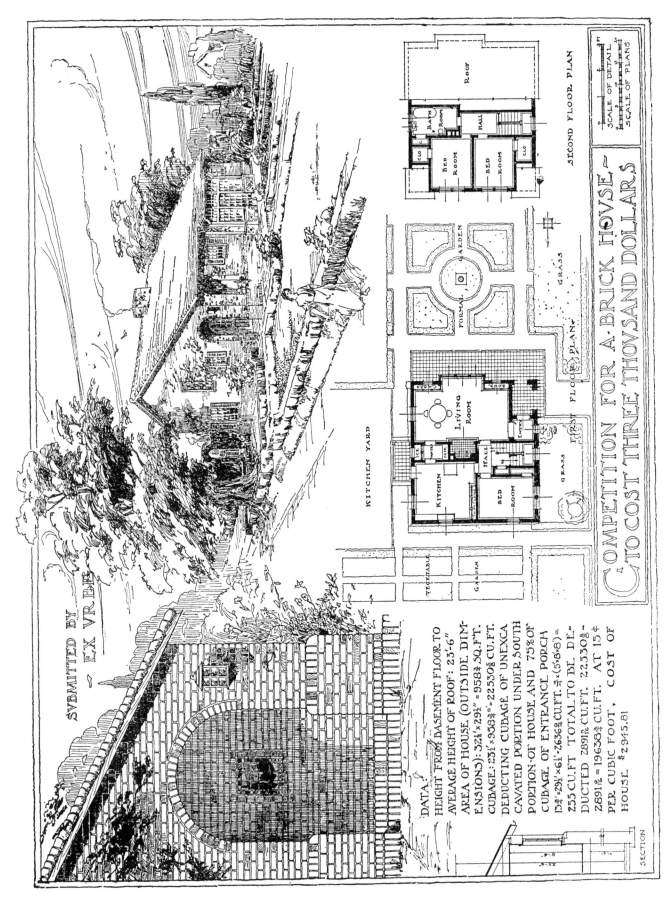

SVBMITTED BY
~ EX VRBE ~

DATA:
HEIGHT FROM BASEMENT FLOOR TO
AVERAGE HEIGHT OF ROOF: 23'-6"
AREA OF HOUSE (OUTSIDE DIM-
ENSIONS): 32¼'×29¼" = 958¾ SQ.FT.
CUBAGE: 23½'×958¾"= 22530⅝ CU.FT.
DEDUCTING CUBAGE OF UNEXCA-
VATED PORTION UNDER SOUTH
PORTION OF HOUSE AND 75% OF
CUBAGE OF ENTRANCE PORCH
13¾'×29¼'×61'-7636½ CU.FT. ¾×(5'×8'×8') =
255 CU.FT TOTAL TO BE DE-
DUCTED 2891½ CU.FT. 22530⅝-
2891½ = 19638¾ CU.FT. AT 15¢
PER CUBIC FOOT, COST OF
HOUSE $2945.81

COMPETITION FOR A·BRICK HOVSE ~
to COST THREE THOVSAND DOLLARS

DESIGN BY HENRY W. HALL & HUGO K. GRAF

SECOND FLOOR PLAN

FIRST FLOOR PLAN

SECTION

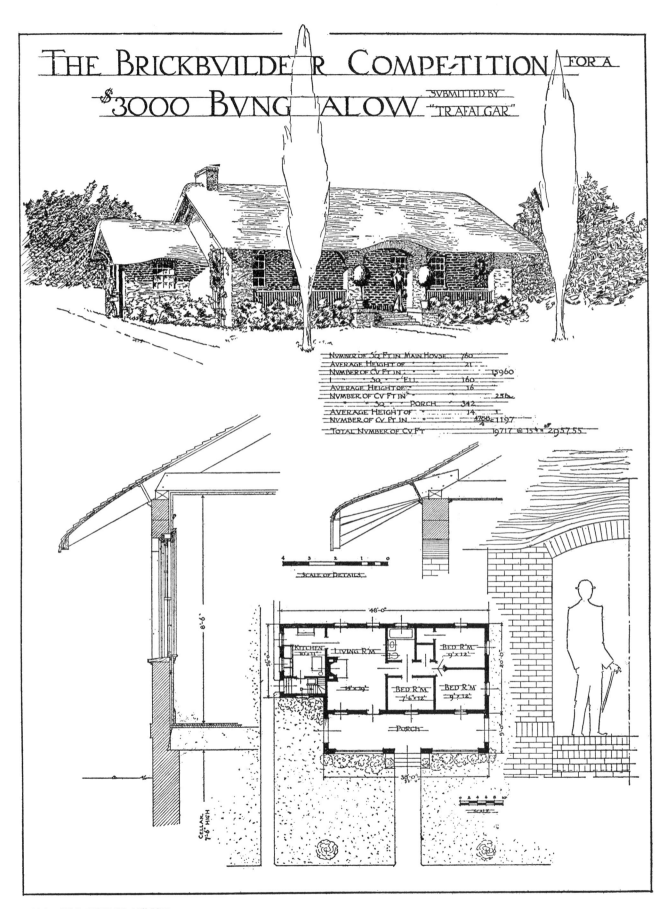

THE BRICKBVILDER COMPETITION FOR A
$3000 BVNGALOW

SVBMITTED BY "TRAFALGAR"

NVMBER OF SQ FT IN MAIN HOVSE	760	
AVERAGE HEIGHT OF "	21	
NVMBER OF CV FT IN "		15960
" SQ " ELL	160	
AVERAGE HEIGHT OF "	16	
NVMBER OF CV FT IN "		2560
" SQ " PORCH	342	
AVERAGE HEIGHT OF "	14	
NVMBER OF CV FT IN "	4788÷4	1197
TOTAL NVMBER OF CV FT	19717 @ 15¢	2957.55

SCALE OF DETAILS

8'-6"

CELLAR 7'-6" HIGH

48'-0"

KITCHEN 10'X11'   LIVING R'M

16'-0"

14'X19'   BED R'M 7'6"X12'   BED R'M 9'X12'

BED R'M 9'X12'

40'-0"

9'-6"

PORCH

38'-0"

SCALE

DESIGN BY F. HOWARD NELSON
50 Bromfield Street, Boston, Mass.

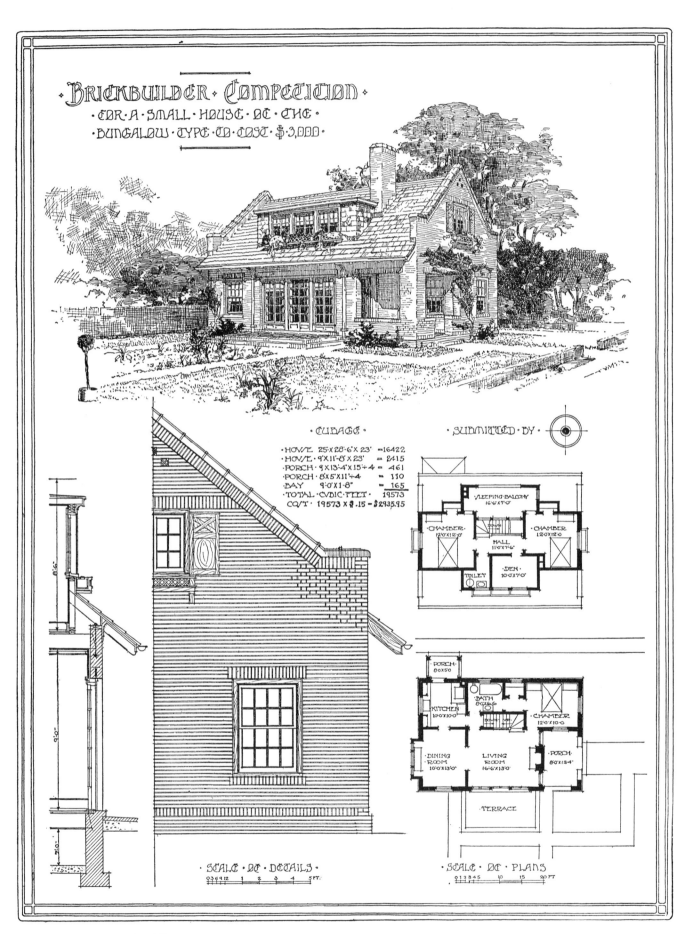

·BRICKBUILDER·COMPETITION·
·FOR·A·SMALL·HOUSE·OF·THE·
·BUNGALOW·TYPE·TO·COST·$·3,000·

·CUBAGE·

·HOVSE· 25'x28'-6"x 23' =16422
·HOVSE· 9'x11'-8"x 23'   = 2415
·PORCH· 9'x13'-4"x15'÷4   = 461
·PORCH· 8'x5'x11'÷4   = 110
·BAY· 9'-0"x1'-8"   = 165
·TOTAL·CVBIC·FEET·   19573
CO/T· 19573 x $.15 =$2935.95

·SUBMITTED·BY·

SLEEPING·BALCONY·
16'-6"x7'-0"

CHAMBER· 12'-0"x12'-0"
CHAMBER· 12'-0"x12'-0"
HALL· 11'-0"x7'-6"
TOILET·
DEN· 10'-0"x7'-0"

PORCH· 8'-0"x5'-0"
KITCHEN· 10'-0"x10'-0"
BATH· 8'-0"x6'-6"
CHAMBER· 12'-0"x10'-0"
DINING·ROOM· 10'-0"x13'-0"
LIVING·ROOM· 16'-6"x13'-0"
PORCH· 8'-0"x12'-4"
TERRACE·

·SCALE·OF·DETAILS·
0 3 6 9 12   1   2   3   4   5 FT.

·SCALE·OF·PLANS·
0 1 2 3 4 5   10   15   20 FT

DESIGN BY WILLIAM R. SCHMITT
104 West 92nd Street, New York, N. Y.

72

DETAILS OF FRONT

DATA FOR ESTIMATING COST
·24'-3" X 45'-0"+3'-4"X20'-0"+7'-8"X20-0 X 13-6 (AVERAGE·HEIGHT·FROM·GRADE·
·TO·CENTER·OF·ROOF = 17701·CU·FT + 320·CU·FT (1/4·VERANDA·AREA·ETC)·
·+ 14'-0" X 20-0"X 7-0" (1960·CU·FT·BAS'M'NT·AREA) = 19981·CU·FT·TOTALS·
·19981·X·.15 = ²997.15·TOTAL·COST

FLOOR PLAN

SECTION·EXTERIOR·WALL·

BRICKBVILDER COMPETITION FOR
A BRICK BVNGALOW TO COST $3000

·SUBMITTED·BY·

DESIGN BY WARNER A. EBBETS
1423 Harvard Street, N. W., Washington, D. C.

73

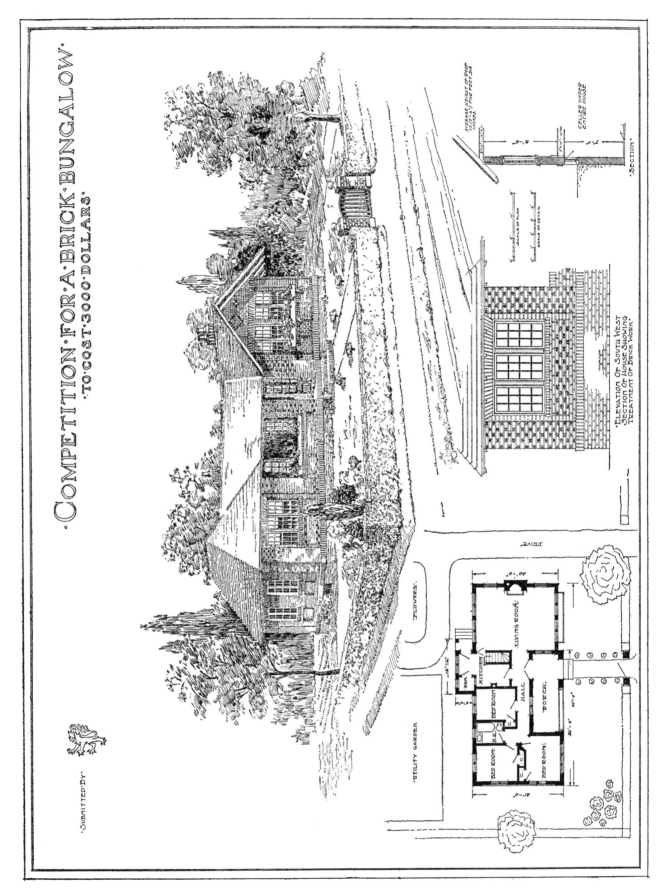

COMPETITION·FOR·A·BRICK·BUNGALOW·
·TO·COST·3000·DOLLARS·

·SUBMITTED·BY·

ELEVATION OF SOUTH WEST
SECTION OF HOUSE SHOWING
TREATMENT OF BRICK WORK·

DESIGN BY WALTER F. KRAFT
57 Clifton Place, Brooklyn, N. Y.

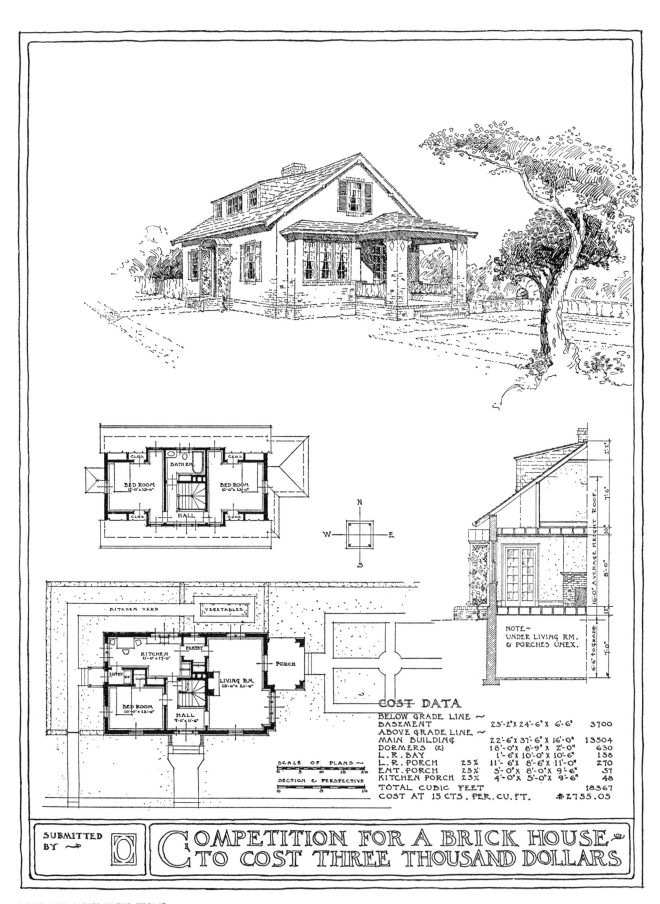

COST DATA

BELOW GRADE LINE ~		
BASEMENT	23'-2" X 24'-6" X 6'-6"	3700
ABOVE GRADE LINE ~		
MAIN BUILDING	22'-6" X 37'-6" X 16'-0"	13504
DORMERS (2)	18'-0" X 8'-9" X 2'-0"	630
L.R. BAY	1'-6" X 10'-0" X 10'-6"	158
L.R. PORCH 25%	11'-6" X 8'-6" X 11'-0"	270
ENT. PORCH 25%	5'-0" X 8'-0" X 9'-6"	57
KITCHEN PORCH 25%	4'-0" X 5'-0" X 9'-6"	48
TOTAL CUBIC FEET		18367
COST AT 15 CTS. PER. CU. FT.		$2755.05

SUBMITTED BY ~

COMPETITION FOR A BRICK HOUSE TO COST THREE THOUSAND DOLLARS

DESIGN BY JAMES HICKS STONE
1401 Chemical Building, St. Louis, Mo.

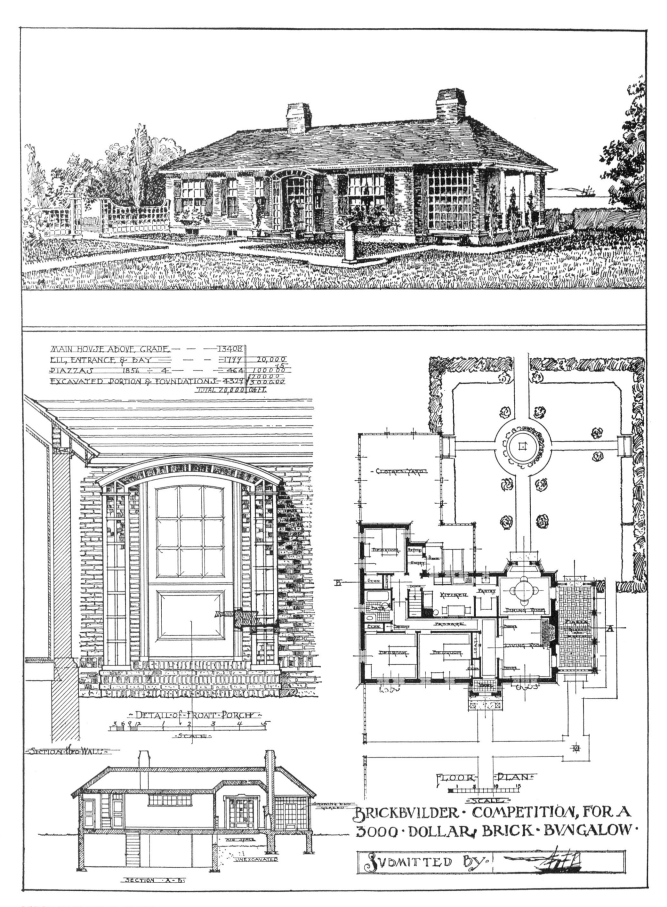

MAIN HOVSE ABOVE GRADE — — 13408
ELL, ENTRANCE & BAY — — 1799 · 20,000
PIAZZAS 1856 ÷ 4 — — 464 · 10000 ·
EXCAVATED PORTION & FOVNDATIONS 4329 · 300600 ·
TOTAL 20,000 CV.FT.

· DETAIL·OF·FRONT·PORCH ·

· SECTION·THRO·WALL ·

SECTION · A · B ·

· CLOISTER·YARD ·

· FLOOR — PLAN ·

BRICKBVILDER · COMPETITION, FOR A
3000 · DOLLAR, BRICK · BVNGALOW ·

SVBMITTED BY:

DESIGN BY FRANK C. ADAMS
3 Hamilton Place, Room 612, Boston, Mass.

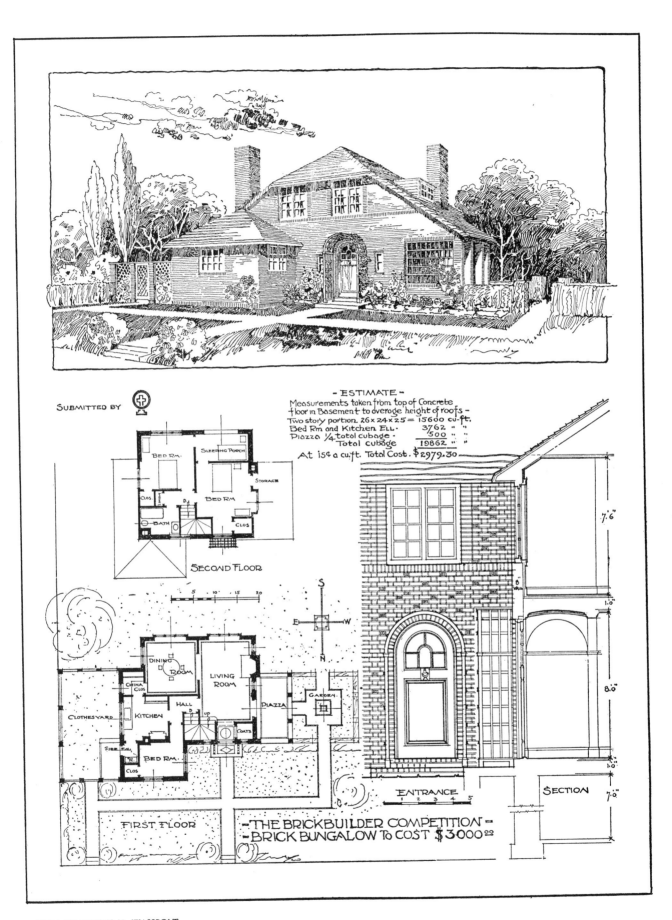

- ESTIMATE -
Measurements taken from top of Concrete
floor in Basement to average height of roofs -
Two story portion 26 x 24 x 25 = 15600 cu-ft.
Bed Rm and Kitchen Ell · 3762 " "
Piazza ¼ total cubage · 500 " "
Total cubage 19862 " "
At 15¢ a cu·ft. Total Cost · $2979.30

SUBMITTED BY

SECOND FLOOR

BED RM.   SLEEPING PORCH

STORAGE

CLOS.   BED RM.

BATH   CLOS.

DINING ROOM   LIVING ROOM

CHINA CLOS.

HALL   PIAZZA   GARDEN.

CLOTHES YARD   KITCHEN

COATS

SER. RM.   BED RM.

CLOS.

FIRST FLOOR

-THE BRICKBUILDER COMPETITION-
-BRICK BUNGALOW TO COST $3000.00

ENTRANCE

SECTION

7'·6"

8'·0"

1'·0"

7'·0"

DESIGN BY ROBERT H. WAMBOLT
3 Hamilton Place, Room 612, Boston, Mass.

PERSPECTIVE·VIEW

BRICKBVILDER·COMPETITION
A·BRICK·BVNGALOW
TO·COST $3000.00
SVBMITTED·BY

FOVNDATION·PLAN

GROVND·FLOOR·PLAN

DIMENSIONS·CVBAGE·&·COST

MAIN·BVILDING	27'x31x14	TOTAL 11718 c.f. — 15 c.r.	$1757.70
CELLAR under portion	16x27x5	2160	324.
EXTENSION each	13x16x12	4992	748.80
CELLAR STAIRS	4x3x5	336	50.40
AREAS each	2x5x5	60	9.
BAY WINDOW	16x11.6x7	121	18.15
TERRACE covered	8x16x11	1408	56.32
" uncovered	8x15x4	480	19.20
KITCHEN·PORCH	4x6x6x4	104	4.16
		TOTAL	$2987.73

DESIGN BY GEORGE G. CROCKETT
436 Convent Avenue, New York, N. Y.

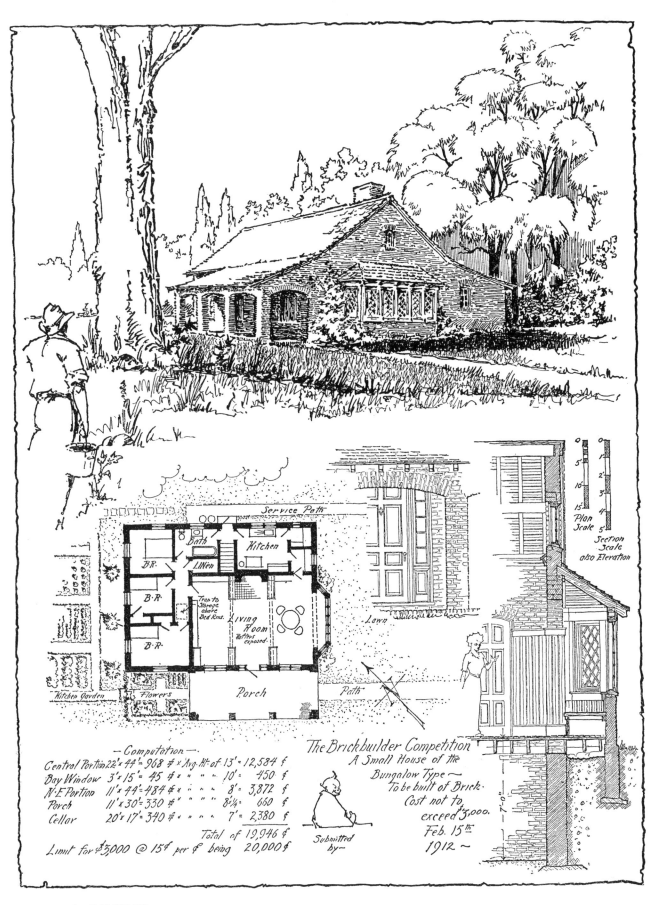

— Computation —
Central Portion 22' x 44' = 968 ♯ x Avg. Ht. of 13' = 12,584 ♯
Bay Window 3' x 15' = 45 ♯ x " " 10' = 450 ♯
N·E Portion 11' x 44' = 484 ♯ x " " 8' = 3,872 ♯
Porch 11' x 30' = 330 ♯ x " " 8'¼ = 660 ♯
Cellar 20' x 17' = 340 ♯ x " " 7' = 2,380 ♯
Total of 19,946 ♯
Limit for $3,000 @ 15¢ per ♯ being 20,000 ♯

Submitted by —

The Brickbuilder Competition
A Small House of the
Bungalow Type —
To be built of Brick.
Cost not to
exceed $3,000.
Feb. 15th
1912 ~

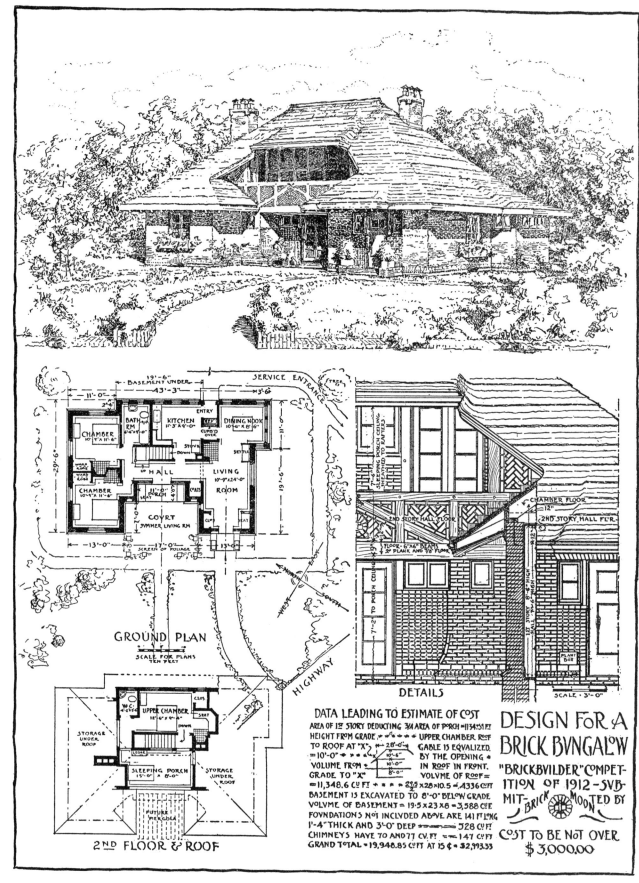

DATA LEADING TO ESTIMATE OF COST

AREA OF 1ST STORY DEDUCTING 3/4 AREA OF PORCH = 1134·55 FT
HEIGHT FROM GRADE UPPER CHAMBER ROOF
TO ROOF AT "X" = 28'-0" GABLE IS EQUALIZED
= 10'-0" BY THE OPENING
VOLUME FROM IN ROOF IN FRONT.
GRADE TO "X" VOLUME OF ROOF =
= 11,348.6 CU FT = 21.5 x28x10.5 = 4336 CUFT
BASEMENT IS EXCAVATED TO 8'-0" BELOW GRADE
VOLUME OF BASEMENT = 19.5 x23 x8 = 3,588 CUE
FOUNDATIONS NOT INCLUDED ABOVE ARE 141 FT LONG
1'-4" THICK AND 3'-0" DEEP = 528 CU FT
CHIMNEYS HAVE 70 AND 77 CU FT = 147 CU FT
GRAND TOTAL = 19,948.85 CU FT AT 15¢ = $2,993.33

DESIGN FOR A BRICK BVNGALOW

"BRICKBVILDER" COMPETITION OF 1912 — SVBMITTED BY BRICK MOONE

COST TO BE NOT OVER $3,000.00

GROUND PLAN

SCALE FOR PLANS
TEN FEET

DETAILS

SCALE · 3'-0"

2ND FLOOR & ROOF

DESIGN BY CHALMERS S. CLAPP
35 Downer Avenue, Dorchester, Mass.

BRICKBUILDER COMPETITION FOR A THREE THOUSAND DOLLAR BUNGALOW TYPE HOUSE

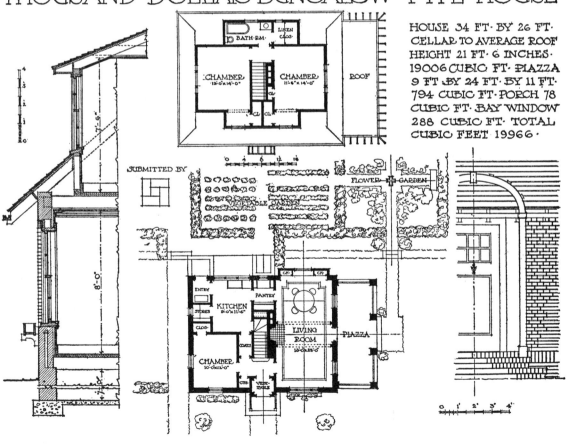

HOUSE 34 FT· BY 26 FT· CELLAR TO AVERAGE ROOF HEIGHT 21 FT· 6 INCHES· 19006 CUBIC FT· PIAZZA 9 FT· BY 24 FT· BY 11 FT· 794 CUBIC FT· PORCH 78 CUBIC FT· BAY WINDOW 288 CUBIC FT· TOTAL CUBIC FEET 19966·

DESIGN BY WILLIAM H. PEARE
15 Beacon Street, Boston, Mass.

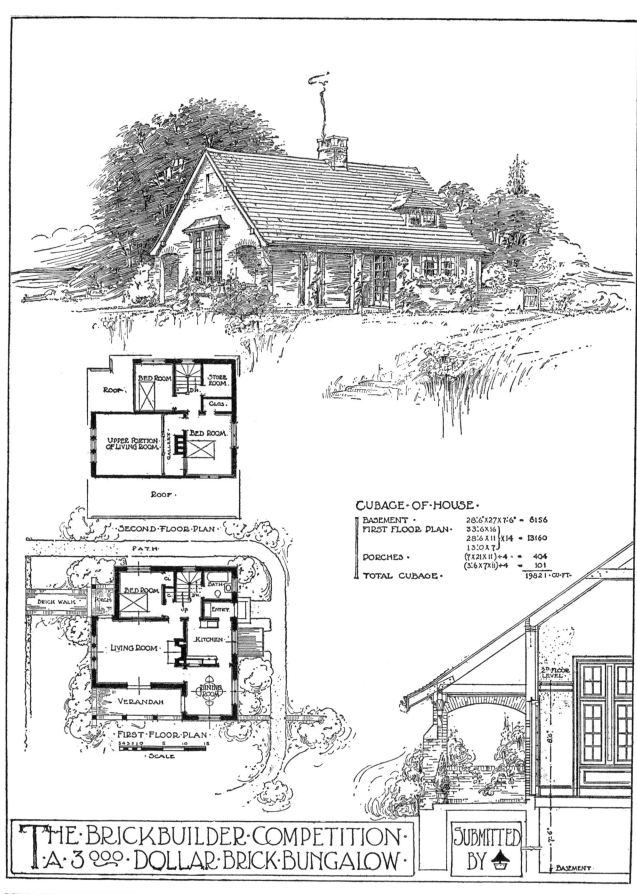

CUBAGE·OF·HOUSE·

BASEMENT · 28:6"X27X7:6" = 6156
FIRST FLOOR PLAN· 33:6X16 }
28:6 X 11 } X14 = 13160
13:0 X 7 }
PORCHES · (7 X 21 X 11) ÷ 4 = 404
(3:6 X 7 X11) ÷ 4 = 101
TOTAL CUBAGE· 19821 · CU·FT·

SECOND·FLOOR·PLAN·

FIRST·FLOOR·PLAN·

·SCALE·

THE·BRICKBUILDER·COMPETITION·
·A·3000·DOLLAR·BRICK·BUNGALOW·

SUBMITTED BY

DESIGN BY MANLY C. BEEBE
1105 Massachusetts Avenue, Cambridge, Mass.

82

SCALE

SUBMITTED·BY·

19400 CUBIC FT·

THE·BRICK·BUILDER·COMPETITION·FOR·A·BRICK·
BUNGALOW·TO·COST·THREE·THOUSAND·DOLLARS·

DESIGN BY·HERBERT G. MASON
9 Park Street, Boston, Mass.

DATA

LENGTH - 42'-0"

WIDTH --- 32'-0"

TOTAL CUBAGE
19248 CU FT

SCALE OF PLANS

COMPETITION FOR A
BRICK BUNGALO

SUBMITTED BY

DESIGN BY C. MELVIN FRANK
123 Deshler Avenue, E., Columbus, Ohio

84

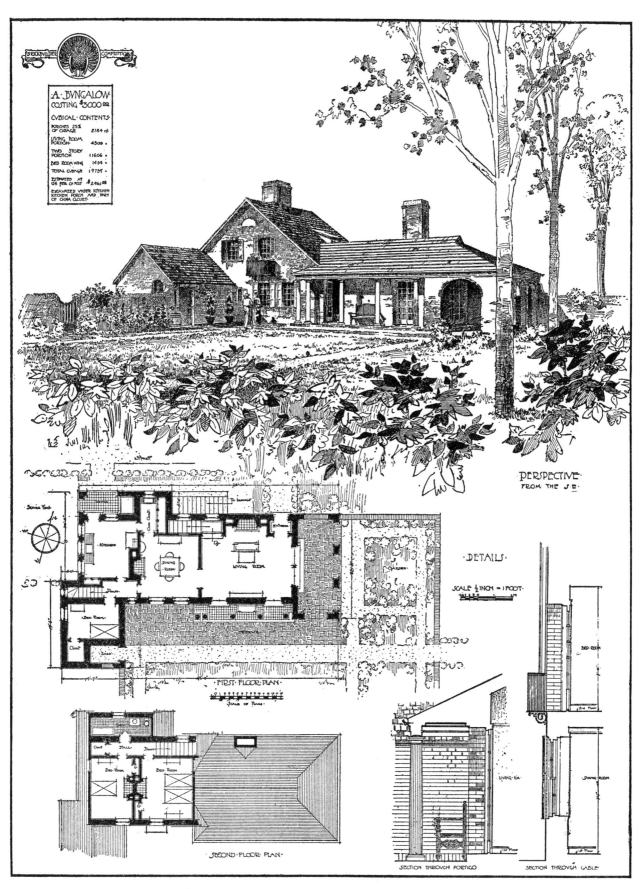

85

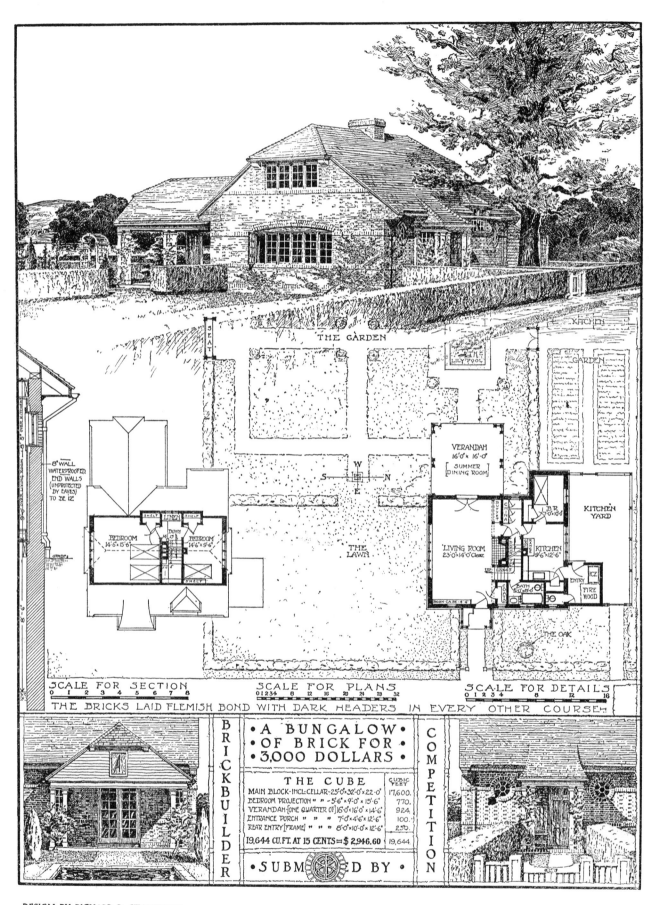

THE GARDEN

SEAT

KITCHEN

THE
LILY POOL

GARDEN

8" WALL
WATERPROOFED
END WALLS
(UNPROTECTED
BY EAVES)
TO BE 12"

VERANDAH
16'-0" x 16'-0"
SUMMER
DINING ROOM

W

S   N

E

BEDROOM
14'-6" x 15'-6"

LINEN

BEDROOM
14'-6" x 9'-6"

DOWN

SHELF   SHELF

SHELF

B.R.
9'-0" x 10'-0"

KITCHEN
YARD

THE
LAWN

LIVING ROOM
23'-0" x 14'-0" Clear.

KITCHEN
9'-6" x 12'-6"

UP

ENTRY

ICE

BATH
5'-0" x 6'-0"

FIRE
WOOD

BOOK-CASE 4'-6"

THE OAK

SCALE FOR SECTION
0 1 2 3 4 5 6 7 8

SCALE FOR PLANS
0 1 2 3 4   8   12   16   20   24   28   32

SCALE FOR DETAILS
0 1 2 3 4   8   12   16

THE BRICKS LAID FLEMISH BOND WITH DARK HEADERS IN EVERY OTHER COURSE

BRICKBUILDER

• A BUNGALOW •
• OF BRICK FOR •
• 3,000 DOLLARS •

THE CUBE

		CUBIC FEET
MAIN BLOCK—INCL: CELLAR—25'-0" x 32'-0" x 22'-0"		17,600.
BEDROOM PROJECTION " " — 5'-6" x 9'-0" x 15'-6"		770.
VERANDAH [ONE QUARTER OF] 16'-0" x 16'-0" x 14'-6"		924.
ENTRANCE PORCH " " 7'-0" x 4'-6" x 12'-6"		100.
REAR ENTRY [FRAME] " " 8'-0" x 10'-0" x 12'-6"		250.
19,644 CU.FT. AT 15 CENTS = $ 2,946.60		19,644.

• SUBMITTED BY •

COMPETITION

DESIGN BY RICHARD R. STANWOOD
189 Bay State Road, Boston, Mass.

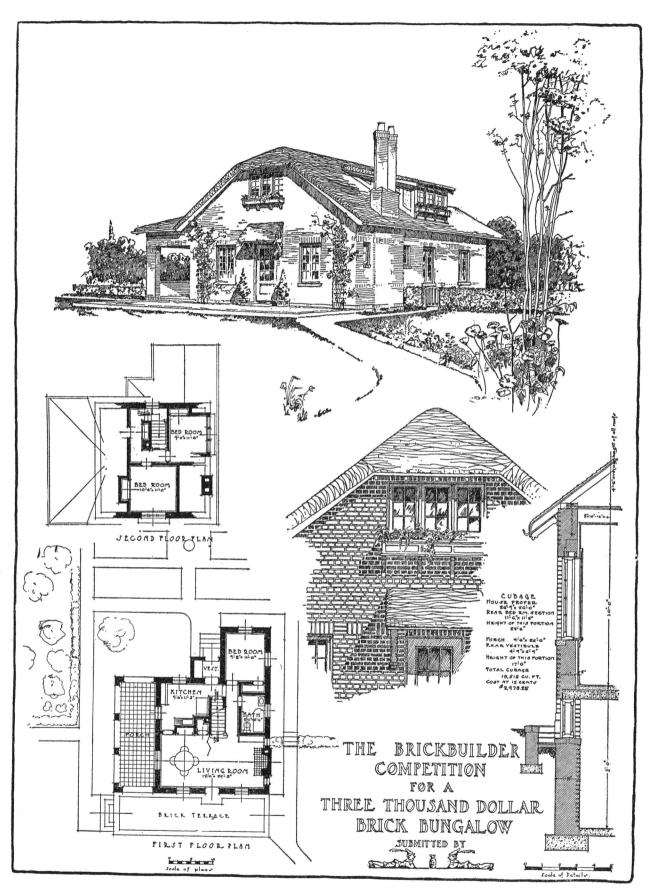

SECOND FLOOR PLAN

BED ROOM
9'-0" x 11'-6"

BED ROOM
10'-6" x 11'-0"

FIRST FLOOR PLAN

BED ROOM
9'-8" x 11'-0"

VEST.

KITCHEN
9'-6" x 11'-3"

BATH

PORCH

LIVING ROOM
13'-0" x 21'-3"

BRICK TERRACE

Scale of plans

CUBAGE
HOUSE PROPER
26'-9" x 26'-0"
REAR BED RM. SECTION
11'-6" x 11'-6"
HEIGHT OF THIS PORTION
22'-6"

PORCH 9'-6" x 22'-0"
REAR VESTIBULE
4'-9" x 6'-9"
HEIGHT OF THIS PORTION
17'-0"
TOTAL CUBAGE
19,815 CU. FT.
COST AT 15 CENTS
$2,973.25

THE BRICKBUILDER
COMPETITION
FOR A
THREE THOUSAND DOLLAR
BRICK BUNGALOW
SUBMITTED BY

Scale of Details.

DESIGN BY FREDERICK S. STOTT & ELMER A. OLBERG
715 Capital Bank Building, St. Paul, Minn.

87

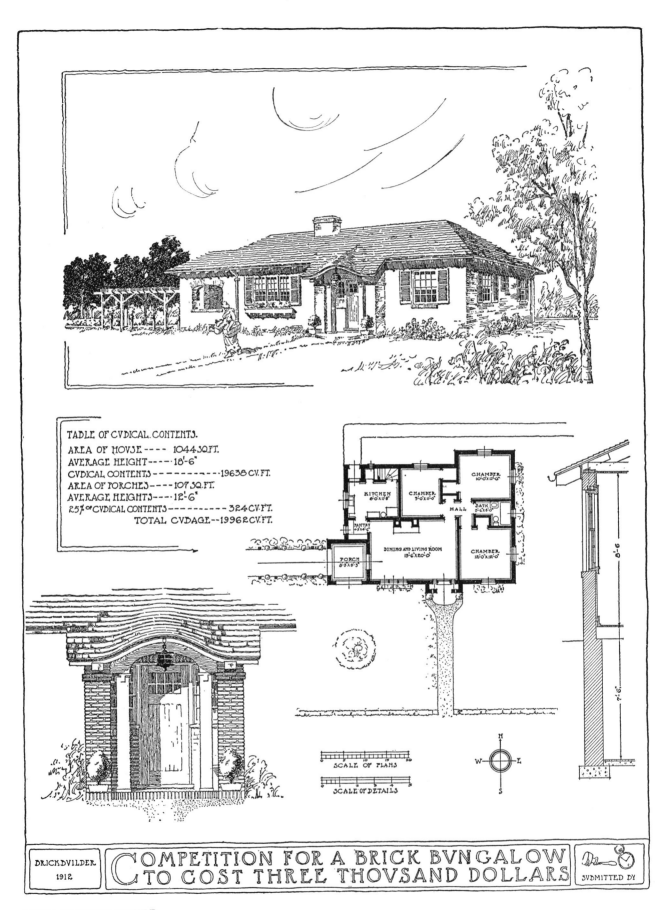

TADLE OF CVDICAL CONTENTS.
AREA OF HOVSE ---- 1044 SQ.FT.
AVERAGE HEIGHT ---- 18'-6"
CVDICAL CONTENTS --------- 19638 CV.FT.
AREA OF PORCHES ---- 107 SQ.FT.
AVERAGE HEIGHTS ---- 12'-6"
25% OF CVDICAL CONTENTS --------- 324 CV.FT.
TOTAL CVDAGE -- 19962 CV.FT.

SCALE OF PLANS

SCALE OF DETAILS

BRICKDVILDER
1912

COMPETITION FOR A BRICK BVNGALOW
TO COST THREE THOVSAND DOLLARS

SVDMITTED DY

DESIGN BY GEORGE SCHMIDT
2719 Orleans Street, Baltimore, Md.

88

A BRICK BUNGALOW ·

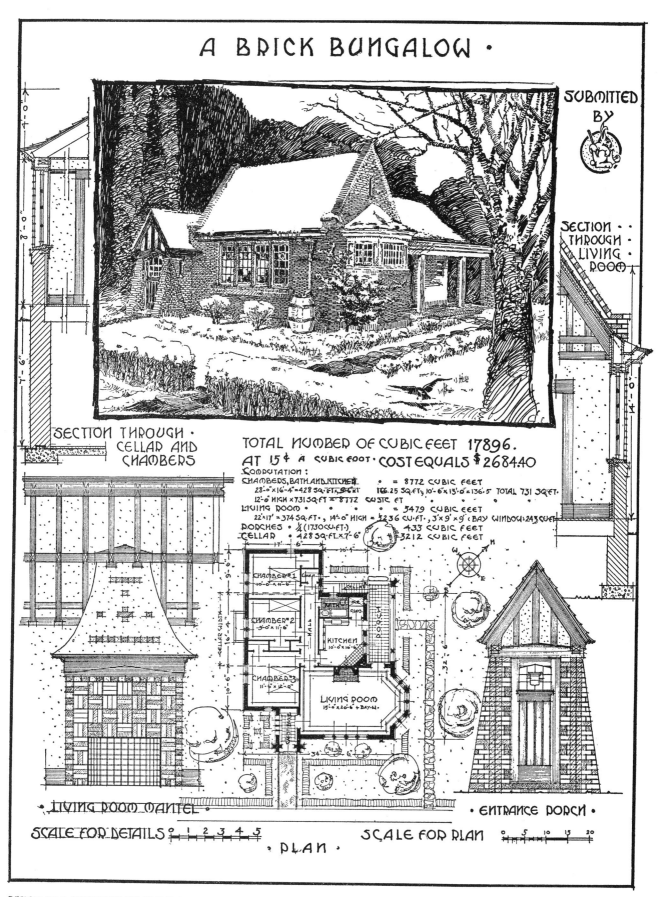

SUBMITTED BY

SECTION · THROUGH · LIVING · ROOM

SECTION THROUGH · CELLAR AND CHAMBERS

TOTAL NUMBER OF CUBIC FEET 17896.
AT 15¢ A CUBIC FOOT· COST EQUALS $2684.40

COMPUTATION:
CHAMBERS, BATH AND KITCHEN · = 8772 CUBIC FEET
28'-0"×16'-4"=428 SQ.FT, 9'-6"×T 166.25 SQ.FT, 10'-6"×13'-0"=136.5 TOTAL 731 SQ.FT.
12'-0" HIGH ×731 SQ.FT = 8772 CU.STC.FT
LIVING ROOM · = 5479 CUBIC FEET
22'×17' = 374 SQ.FT , 14'-0" HIGH = 5236 CU.FT, 3'×9'×9' BAY WINDOW 243 CU.FT
PORCHES · ¼ (1730 CU.FT.) 433 CUBIC FEET
CELLAR · 428 SQ.FT×7'-6" 3212 CUBIC FEET

CHAMBER 1
10'-0"×11'-6"

CHAMBER 2
9'-0"×11'-6"

KITCHEN
10'-6"×10'-6"

CHAMBER 3
11'-6"×12'-0"

LIVING ROOM
15'-0"×20'-6" + BAY-W.

CELLAR WIDTH 16'-4"

· LIVING ROOM MANTEL ·

· ENTRANCE PORCH ·

SCALE FOR DETAILS 0 1 2 3 4 5

SCALE FOR PLAN 0 5 10 15 20

· PLAN ·

DESIGN BY J. THEODORE HANEMANN
103 Park Avenue, New York, N. Y.

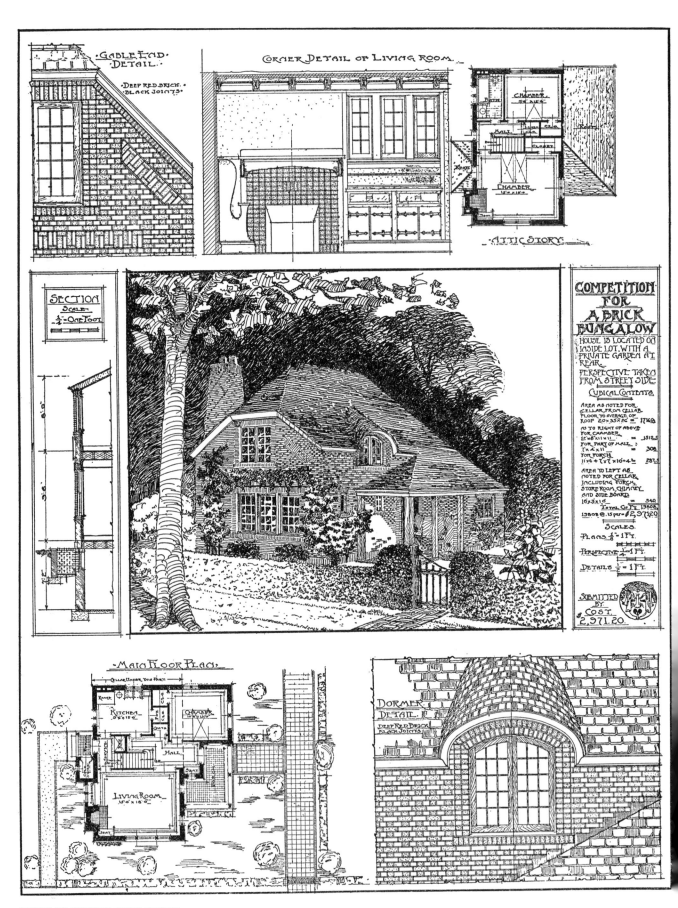

·GABLE END·
DETAIL·

· DEEP RED BRICK ·
BLACK JOINTS·

CORNER DETAIL OF LIVING ROOM·

·ATTIC STORY·

SECTION
SCALE
¼"=ONE FOOT

COMPETITION
FOR
A BRICK
BUNGALOW
HOUSE IS LOCATED ON
INSIDE LOT, WITH A
PRIVATE GARDEN AT
REAR·

PERSPECTIVE TAKEN
FROM STREET SIDE·

CUBICAL CONTENTS·

SCALES·

PLANS ⅛"=1FT·

PERSPECTIVE ¼"=1FT·

DETAILS ½"=1FT·

SUBMITTED
BY
COST·
$2,971.20·

·MAIN FLOOR PLAN·

KITCHEN

CHAMBER

HALL

LIVING ROOM

DORMER
DETAIL·

DEEP RED BRICK
BLACK JOINTS·

DESIGN BY WILLIAM JOHN CHERRY
103 Park Avenue, New York, N. Y.

90

DESIGN BY ARTHUR V. JORY
1420 Spring Street, Berkeley, Cal.

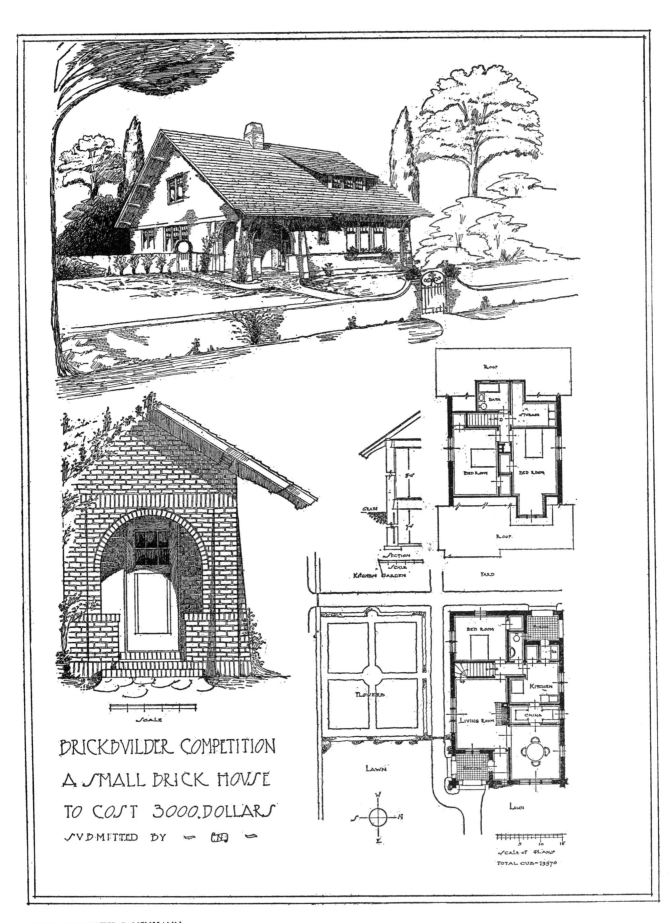

BRICKBVILDER COMPETITION
A SMALL BRICK HOVSE
TO COST 3000. DOLLARS
SVBMITTED BY

DESIGN BY WALTER F. NEUMANN
1089 26th Street, Milwaukee, Wis.

92

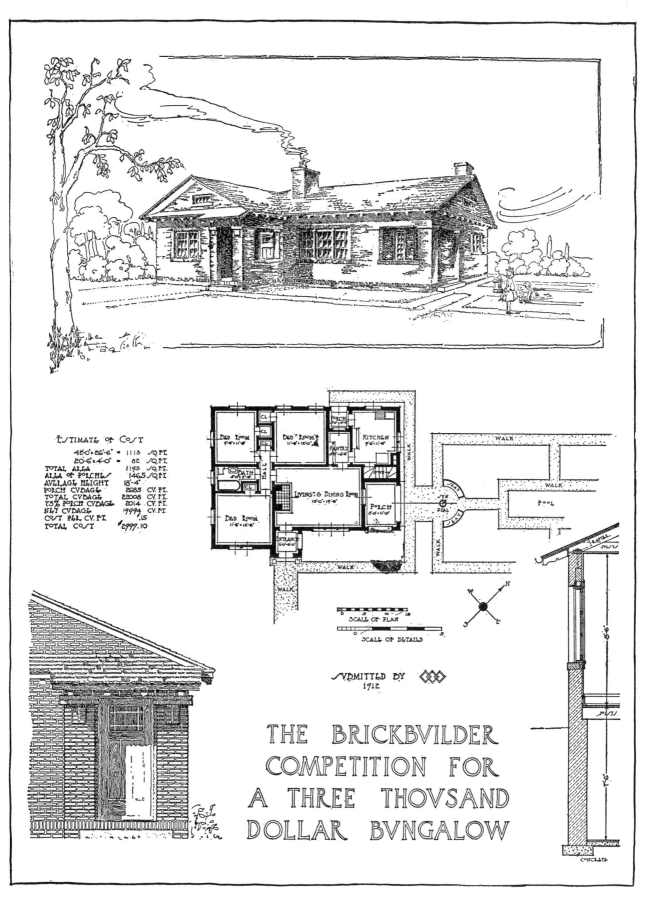

ESTIMATE OF COST

46'-0"x26'-6" = 1113 SQ FT.
20'-6"x4'-0" = 82 SQ FT.
TOTAL AREA   1195 SQ FT.
AREA OF PORCHES   146.5 SQ FT.
AVERAGE HEIGHT   18'-4"
PORCH CUBAGE   2683 CV FT.
TOTAL CUBAGE   22008 CV FT.
75% PORCH CUBAGE 2014 CV FT.
NET CUBAGE   19994 CV FT.
COST PER CV FT.   .15
TOTAL COST $2999.10

SUBMITTED BY
1912

THE BRICKBVILDER
COMPETITION FOR
A THREE THOVSAND
DOLLAR BVNGALOW

DESIGN BY HOWARD G. HALL
1619 Harlem Avenue, Baltimore, Md.

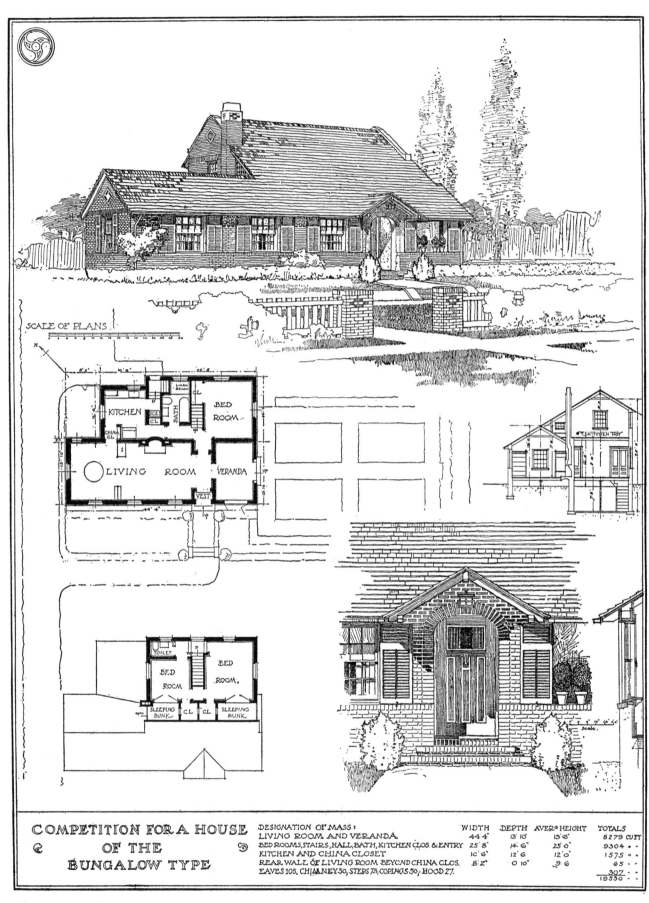

SCALE OF PLANS

LINEN BELOW

KITCHEN

ICE

CL

CHINA CL

BATH

BED ROOM

S

LIVING ROOM

VERANDA

VEST

KITCHEN HGT

TOILET

BED ROOM

BED ROOM

SLEEPING BUNK

CL

CL

SLEEPING BUNK

Scale.

COMPETITION FOR A HOUSE
OF THE
BUNGALOW TYPE

DESIGNATION OF MASS:	WIDTH	DEPTH	AVER? HEIGHT	TOTALS
LIVING ROOM AND VERANDA	44'4"	13'10"	13'8"	8279 CU FT
BED ROOMS, STAIRS, HALL, BATH, KITCHEN CLOS. & ENTRY	25'8"	14'6"	25'0"	9304 " "
KITCHEN AND CHINA CLOSET	16'6"	12'6"	12'0"	1575 " "
REAR WALL OF LIVING ROOM BEYOND CHINA CLOS.	8'2"	0'10"	9'6"	65 " "
EAVES 105, CHIMNEY 50, STEPS 75, COPINGS 50, HOOD 27.				307 " "
				19530

DESIGN BY J. T. TUBBY, JR.
81 Fulton Street, New York, N. Y.

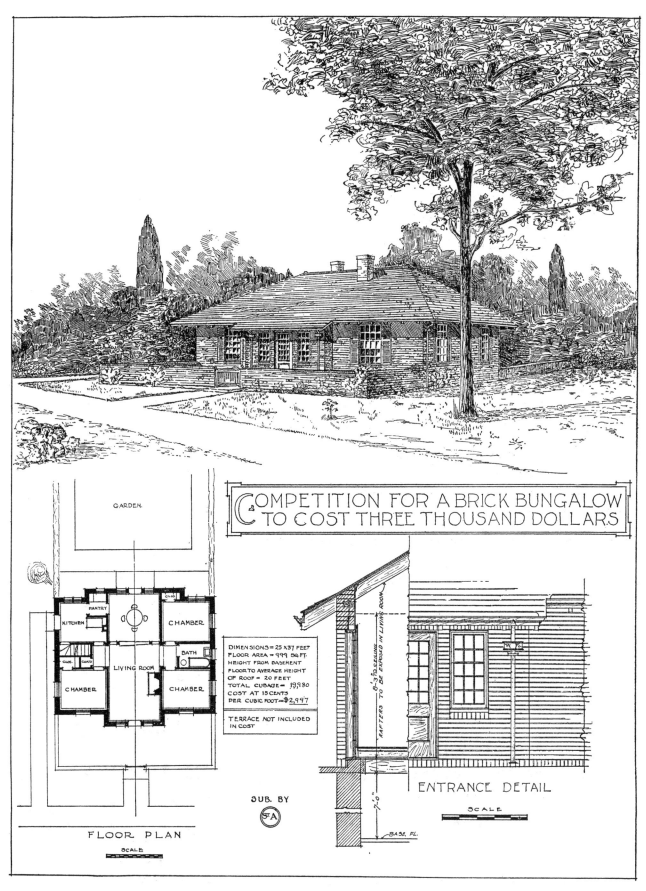

COMPETITION FOR A BRICK BUNGALOW TO COST THREE THOUSAND DOLLARS.

GARDEN.

PANTRY

KITCHEN

CLOS.

CHAMBER

BATH

CLOS. COATS

LIVING ROOM

CHAMBER

CHAMBER

DIMENSIONS = 25 X 37 FEET
FLOOR AREA = 999 SQ. FT.
HEIGHT FROM BASEMENT
FLOOR TO AVERAGE HEIGHT
OF ROOF = 20 FEET
TOTAL CUBAGE = 19,980
COST AT 15 CENTS
PER CUBIC FOOT = $2,997

TERRACE NOT INCLUDED
IN COST

SUB. BY

S⁺A

8'-3" TO CEILING

RAFTERS TO BE EXPOSED IN LIVING ROOM

7'-0"

BASE. FL.

ENTRANCE DETAIL

SCALE

FLOOR PLAN

SCALE

DESIGN BY ALBERT M. KREIDER & EDWIN B. HAXTON
89 Franklin Street, Boston, Mass.

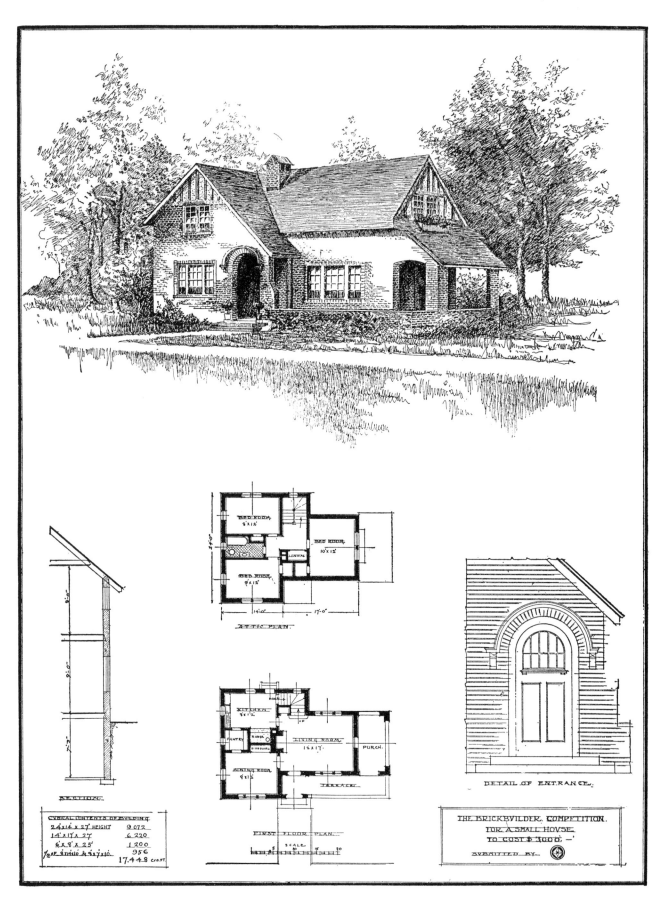

SECTION.

CUBICAL CONTENTS OF BUILDING.
24'x14 x 27' HEIGHT   9 072
14'x17'x 27'   6 220
6'x 8' x 25'   1 200
½ OF 8'x14'10 & 9'x7'x10   956
                          17.448 CUB.FT

ATTIC PLAN.

BED ROOM
9'x12'

BED ROOM
10'x12'

BED ROOM
9'x12'

FIRST FLOOR PLAN.

KITCHEN
8'x12'

PANTRY

LIVING ROOM
12'x17'

PORCH.

DINING ROOM
9'x12'

TERRACE.

SCALE

DETAIL OF ENTRANCE.

THE BRICKBVILDER. COMPETITION.
FOR A SMALL HOVSE
TO COST $3000 —
SVBMITTED BY

DESIGN BY ROBERT L. STEVENSON
346 Fourth Avenue, New York, N. Y.

96

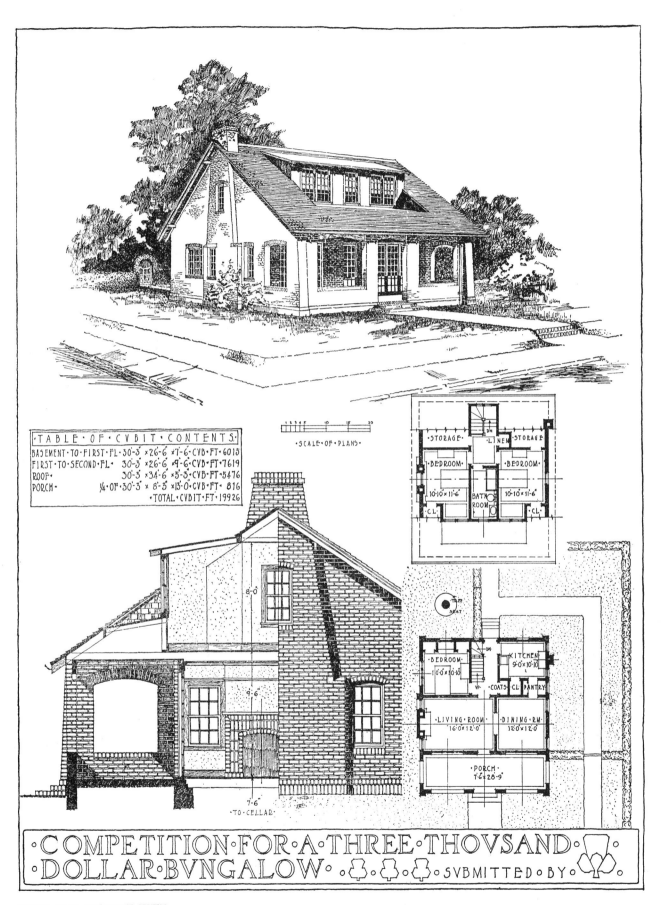

TABLE·OF·CVBIT·CONTENTS·
BASEMENT·TO·FIRST·FL·30-3 ×26-6 ×7-6·CVB·FT·6015
FIRST·TO·SECOND·FL· 30-3 ×26-6 ×9-6·CVB·FT·7619
ROOF·   30-3 ×34-6 ×5-3·CVB·FT·5476
PORCH·   ¼·OF·30-3 × 8-3 ×13-0·CVB·FT· 816
·TOTAL·CVBIT·FT·19926

·SCALE·OF·PLANS·

STORAGE   LINEN   STORAGE
BEDROOM   BATH   BEDROOM
10-10×11-6 ROOM   10-10×11-6
CL   CL

TREE SEAT

BEDROOM   KITCHEN
10-0×10-10   9-0×10-10

COATS·CL PANTRY

LIVING·ROOM   DINING·RM
16-0×12-0   12-0×12-0

PORCH
7-6×28-9

8-0

9-6

7-6
·TO·CELLAR·

·COMPETITION·FOR·A·THREE·THOVSAND·
·DOLLAR·BVNGALOW· ♧ ♧ ♧ ·SVBMITTED·BY·

DESIGN BY T. LOCKHART SMITH
161 W. 11th Avenue, Columbus, Ohio

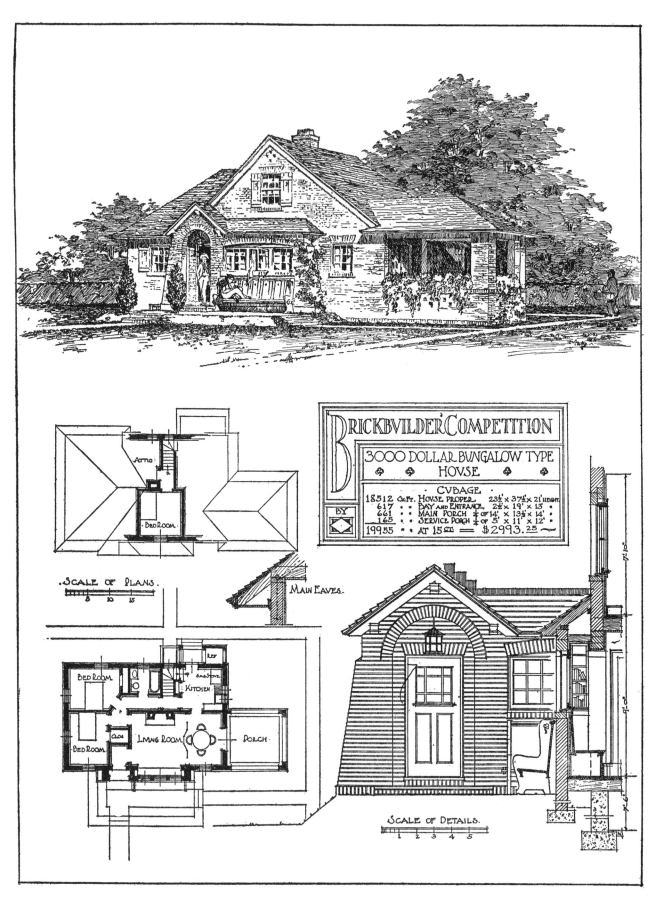

BRICKBVILDER COMPETITION

3000 DOLLAR BUNGALOW TYPE HOVSE

· CVBAGE ·

18512	Cu.Ft.	HOVSE PROPER	23½' x 37½' x 21' HEIGHT.
617	" "	BAY and ENTRANCE	2½' x 19' x 13'
661	" "	MAIN PORCH	½ of 14' x 13½' x 14'
165	" "	SERVICE PORCH	½ of 5' x 11' x 12'
19955	" "	AT 15 CT	= $2993.25

BY

SCALE OF PLANS.
5 10 15

MAIN EAVES.

ATTIC

BED ROOM

BED ROOM

KITCHEN

GAS STOVE

REF

LIVING ROOM

PORCH

BED ROOM

CLOS.

SCALE OF DETAILS.
1 2 3 4 5

DESIGN BY ROBERT W. MAUST
389 N. Grove Street, East Orange, N. J.

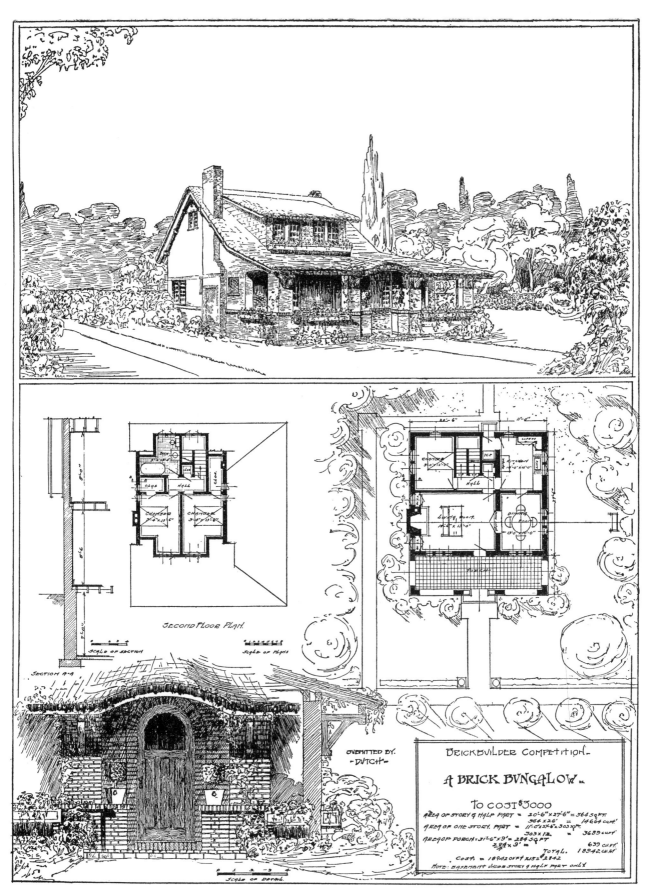

SECOND FLOOR PLAN.

SECTION A·A

SCALE OF SECTION

SCALE OF PLANS

SCALE OF DETAIL.

SUBMITTED BY.
·DVTCH·

BRICKBVILDER COMPETITION·

A BRICK BVNGALOW

TO COST $5000

AREA OF STORY & HALF PART = 20'-6" x 27'-6" = 564 SQ FT.
564 x 26' = 14664 CU FT'
AREA OF ONE STORY. PART = 11'-0"x27'-6"=303 SQ FT.
303 x 12. = 3636 CU FT'
AREA OF PORCH = 31'-6" x 9' = 284 SQ FT
2 84 x 9' = 639 CU FT.
3
TOTAL 18942 CU FT
COST = 18942 CU FT X 15¢ = $2842
NOTE : BASEMENT VNDER STORY & HALF PART ONLY

DESIGN BY R. E. SLUYTER
Herkimer, N. Y.

COMPETITION FOR A SMALL
· BRICK HOUSE ·
OF THE BUNGALOW TYPE COST NOT
TO EXCEED $3,000
~ DATA ~
KITCHEN WING & ENTRY	7190 CU.FT.
BED ROOM WING	7208 "
CENTRAL BAY	5130 "
PORCHES-STEPS-ETC.	472 " "
TOTAL	20000 " "
COST PER CU.FT.	.15
COST OF HOUSE.	$3,000.00

NOTE: FOUNDATION UNDER BED ROOM
WING ONLY GOES DOWN 4'-0" BELOW GRADE,
THIS IS INTIRELY EXCAVATED & FLOOR
COVERED WITH 4" OF CONCRETE.
HOUSE HEATED WITH HOT AIR.

NOM-DE-PLUME

SCALE OF PLAN.

TYPICAL SECTION
THRU CORNICE &
WINDOW HEADS.
SCALE OF CORNICE.

SCALE OF SECTION.

SECTION THRU LIVING RM.
SHOWING BRICK FIRE
PLACE.

DESIGN BY EMIL B. MEYER
318 Union Avenue, Mt. Vernon, N. Y.

CHAMBER
13'-0"x 7'-6"

CLOS

TOILET

HALL

TRUNK

CLOS

CHAMBER
13'-0"x 9'-6"

SEAT

ATTIC AND ROOF PLAN

PERSPECTIVE VIEW
SCALE

CHAMBER
BUILT IN

TABLE RANGE

VESTI-
BULE

PASSAGE

KITCHEN
13'-0"x 7'-6"

CLOS

UP

VESTIBULE

PERGOLA

LIVING & DINING ROOM
28'-0"x 12'-6"

PORCH

FIRST FLOOR PLAN
SCALE

SUBMITTED
BY

DETAIL OF ENTRANCE
SCALE

SECTION

DESIGN BY OLOF DANIELS
33-34 McSaba Block, Duluth, Minn.

Second Floor Plan

Estimate of cost
23·8 X 18·6 X 24·0 = 10524
23·6 X 14·4 X 24·0 = 7916
23·8 X 5·0 X 18·0 = 520
18960
18960 Cubic feet @
15 ¢ per ft = $ 2844·00
terrace & walks 150·00
Total Cost $ 2994·00

Section

First Floor Plan

Detail

Brickbuilder Competition
A house to cost 3,000 Dollars

DESIGN BY A. D. HILL
257 N. Craig Street, Pittsburgh, Pa.

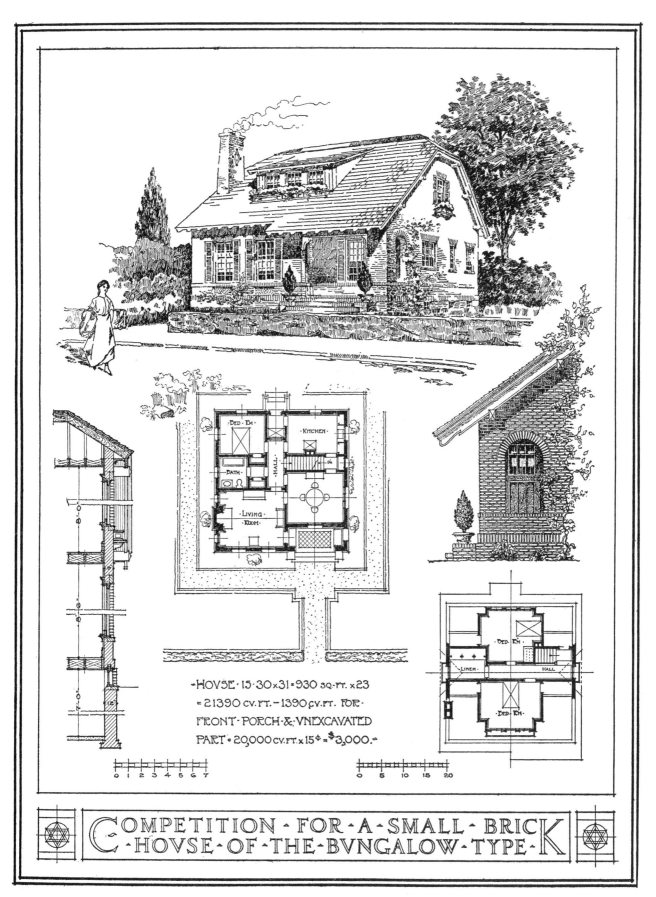

·HOVSE·15·30x31·930·SQ·FT·x23·
= 21390 CV.FT.—1390 CV.FT. FOR·
FRONT·PORCH·&·VNEXCAVATED
PART = 20,000 CV.FT. x 15¢ = $3,000.

0 1 2 3 4 5 6 7

0 5 10 15 20

COMPETITION · FOR · A · SMALL · BRICK
HOVSE · OF · THE · BVNGALOW · TYPE

DESIGN BY FRANK HAUSHKA
10,011 Flora Avenue, Cleveland, Ohio

103

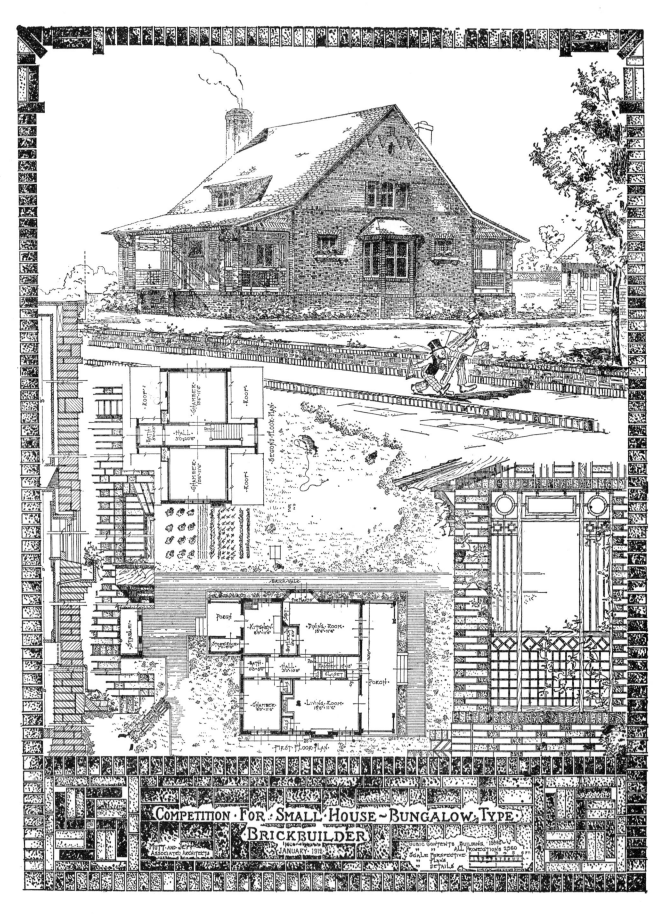

COMPETITION·FOR·SMALL·HOUSE~BUNGALOW·TYPE·
·BRICKBUILDER·
·JANUARY·1912·

MUTT·AND·JEFF·
ASSOCIATED·ARCHITECTS·

The Tale Of An Unbeliever.

ORIGINAL COST.

LET us talk common sense, Philip," I said, with that wise feeling of the man who is soon to take unto himself a wife. "You talk glowingly of Beauty and Permanence and Solidity and all those splendid abstractions. You puff out great clouds of smoke, and half shut your eyes, and see wonderful things. But I'm not interested in dream-creations now. I'm not rearing a Castle in Spain. I've got to build a house and pay for it."

Huntington puffed on and said nothing. We were sitting in that most unromantic of all places on earth, the front parlor of a boarding-house. I had been living there for economy's sake, that I might accumulate enough capital to give me the privilege of making a mortgage to some affluent owner of real estate. And we were earnestly seeking to discover some way in which one dollar could be made to do the work of two.

"Remember the saying of a late President of the United States," I went on airily, "it is a condition we confront, not a theory. I am violating no confidence when I tell you I've saved up just seventeen hundred and seventy-five dollars, and what I want is a simple, unpretentious house, a place to live in, that will keep out the rain and the wind — and possibly mosquitoes and flies if I can afford wire nets for the windows."

Huntington was a quiet, unagressive sort of man, a little gray around the temples, with a rather dried-up face, a fugitive smile, and withal a singularly convincing way about him.

"I went out to the suburbs Sunday, out to Crestwood," he said lazily, as if he had paid little attention to my remarks. "Stayed all day with Hilton. He had just finished painting his frame house. The job — two good coats — cost him a hundred and forty dollars."

He paused a moment to let that sink in, then sat up in his chair, put aside his indolent manner and began to speak in the brisk, even tone of one who was sure of his ground.

"As you say, Harry, it's a condition you face, not a theory. And what you're most concerned about now is the immediate cost of your home. What's going to happen five years from now is not taking up much of your thoughts. It ought to, of course, but we'll come to that later. We'll consider original cost now. Do you know what's the difference in cost between a brick and a frame house?"

"Oh, from twenty to thirty per cent.," I replied carelessly. "Anything but frame is quite out of the question for me."

He leaned forward and shook his long thin finger at me.

"That's just the trouble with you young cock-sure fellows," he said. "You heard somebody say something like that when you were about four and a half years old, and it got stuck in a corner of your brain, and you can't get rid of it. You haven't taken the trouble to look into the matter — you just think a statement you've repeated often enough is a self-evident fact."

"I'm properly rebuked. I give you credit for a crushing introduction. Now go ahead."

"Well, in the first place, did it ever occur to you that the exterior, enclosing walls of a house represent a very small part of its cost? A cost entirely out of proportion to their importance? It is the interior of a house that you spend the bulk of your money on — the partitions and the stairs and the hardwood floors, and the mantel-pieces and the cozy corners and the plumbing and heating and the thousand and one frills and fancies. But it is the outside walls that establish the character of your home, that make it temporary or permanent, cold or warm, a sapping, wearying loss or a lasting prize.

"It is not merely the building laws that are responsible for the brick in the hotels and office buildings and shops you see on city streets. It is the hard business sense of cool, canny business men. They are building for investment, for the future. Were there no building laws they would still scorn frame construction as unspeakable folly."

"But I'm not a millionaire merchant or real estate operator," I interrupted. "I'm a pauper, relatively speaking, and I'm going to get married, and I must have a house that'll come within the sum I have plus the sum I can borrow."

Huntington fell back into his languid, reflective mood for a moment, and blew out a cloud of smoke. "Ah, there's the story," he said musingly. "These cool canny business men are not suffused by the glow of approaching matrimony. They don't have to hold back part of their money for a ring with a big glittering diamond." He laughed, and dropped his pensive manner as suddenly as he had assumed it.

"Tommyrot you're talking, Harry," he went on. "The cold truth is that in a house that can be built for six or seven thousand dollars the difference in first cost between brick and wood walls is not more than five or six hundred dollars. Some say it is less, but that's conservative. Any capitalist who's lending on residences if he knows his business, would rather lend forty-five hundred dollars on a brick house than four thousand on a frame house. And money lenders usually know their business pretty well — you can count on that. Just take a little trouble to inquire into it, and to ask all about brick from those who know, and you can get the exact facts and figures.

"Is there any investment in the world more important than a man's home? If it's all in the world he has, it is so much the more important. It ought to be a religion with him to make it as strong and durable as it can be made. The difference in the cost now, compared with the difference in ultimate results, is as nothing. One day you will appreciate this vividly if you choose brick. And you will appreciate it still more vividly — and with profound sadness — if you do not. For I've come into contact with some of these regrets, and I am convinced that if all the woe that men have suffered from ill-built houses could be piled up together it would equip a deeper hell than Dante ever dreamed of."

The Tale Of An Unbeliever. THE UP-KEEP.

THE next time we talked of my future home — it was about a week after he delivered that first lecture on the folly of flimsy construction — Huntington and I were walking through a neat little suburb. Everything was new — the houses, the spick-and-span grassplots, the curbstones and hydrants and even the trees. The freshly-painted clapboardings fairly glistened in the sun, and the whole village looked as if it had been suddenly lifted out of a show window.

"These houses look good to me, Philip," I said. I was still an unbeliever, but a curious one, waiting to see what new fancies my friend would lay before me.

"I've no doubt the company that built 'em thinks so, too," he said. "This suburb's evidently a thorough success. The houses were built to sell — and they are selling. Still there's always room for one more innocent, and I've no doubt they'll find a place for you."

He had a way of offering a bit of this gentle irony as a foretaste to serious advice. It was a sort of oil for his mental machinery.

"I told you about my friend Hilton's outlay for painting. That house" — pointing to the nearest one — "will need repainting in five years. And another repainting in another five years. A hundred and fifty dollars each time. Thirty dollars a year — the interest on five hundred dollars at 6 per cent. Brick never needs to be painted."

Repainting had always been a vague, far-away contingency in my mind; a future possibility, never a reality. It seemed very brutal of Huntington, like bringing a death's head to a feast, to lug in such a disagreeable thought on such a balmy, sunshiny day. He noticed my displeased expression and chuckled. Then he turned serious.

"That one item alone is enough to make up for the difference in cost," he continued, "but it is only one of many. The saving in insurance premiums is just as marked. The rate for a brick-walled dwelling on the average lot in Chicago — and the same is true of other places — is 30 cents less per $100 than the rate on a wooden-walled dwelling. This applies to contents as well, and means a difference of $15.00 for $5,000 of insurance. At 6 per cent. that represents a capital of $250. But that's merely the financial side of it. You can't value in terms of money the protection that solid construction gives to the lives of you and your family and perhaps to priceless papers and heirlooms and keepsakes.

"About repairs no one can ever give accurate figures in advance. Each house is a problem by itself. But of one thing you can be sure — as soon as a frame house has left the first bloom of youth, so to speak, the mending begins. And it never stops until the house is burned up or falls to pieces like the wonderful one-horse shay. The wood shrinks, swells and warps intermittently. Cold and wind combine to draw the nails by contraction or loosen them by shaking. Decay flourishes unseen behind painted surfaces, and moisture penetrates the least opening. And all manner of vermin will delight to dwell with you if you dwell in a house of wood."

A wise thought occurred to me.

"But the taxes," I said; "they tax you more if you have a brick house."

"That's a point for you," Huntington readily admitted, and then added, "on the surface. But not much of a point when you look deeper. In the first place, the difference is trivial compared to the superiority of your brick house over your neighbor's wooden one. And if you keep to the simple and substantial, as a man of taste should, eschewing the showy and ornate, you'll find the assessor won't be severe on you. In the second place, cities and boroughs are going to wake up some day to the folly of penalizing good construction and putting a premium upon flimsiness. They are going to encourage common-sense building by low taxation and discourage unsafe building by high taxation. That's a prophecy, but it's a reasonable one. Wait and see."

"Well, I suppose you have exhausted all the virtues of your beloved brick now."

"By no means. And I'm not going to try today. But I want you now to consider the heating. Never thought of that? Of course not — it's springtime, and the sun is keeping the mercury at about seventy-five, and you're going to get married. Why worry about coal-bills? But you'll have to next winter, just like ordinary long-married mortals. If you have brick walls about you the heating will cost you probably twenty-five per cent. less than if your house is frame. And remember, this is not an expense for one year only; it's always to be met, as unescapable as death and taxes. Akin to it, but less calculable, is the doctor's bill. With the same constitutions to begin with, the man, wife and children who live within brick walls invariably enjoy better health than those who do not. Good health is the dearest of all possessions, the necessary prerequisite for happiness. But it is more. It is a material blessing, and the man who preserves it is obeying literally the injunction that Roderigo received from the villainous Iago: 'Put money in thy purse.'"

"An alluring picture you paint, truly," I suggested, maybe a little peevish at learning of things I had never even thought to ask questions about before.

"A picture that's not overdrawn, though. What I tell you is not only truth, but it is truth that can be demonstrated. The man who builds of brick is building for all time. His material never wears out, never grows one whit weaker, and it saves him money every year of his life. On the other hand, if he makes wood his choice his home is a never-ending drain. Why, I tell you, Harry," Huntington wheeled me around and we started back to catch our city-bound train — "I tell you I can almost pick out a man who's lived in a frame house over ten years by the hunted look on his face. He looks as if he is just waiting for his wife to say: "John, dear, you'll have to send for the carpenter this morning — we've got to have some new boards where the water leaked in by the chimney on the south side of the house."

The Tale Of An Unbeliever.   BEAUTY THAT LASTS.

THAT was a new suburb we walked through last Sunday," said Huntington, "a kind of Spotless Town put together for show-and-sale purposes. Now we'll see an old place that grew naturally, that used to stand on its own feet as a village long before it became a refuge for weary commuters."

Again we had been talking about my home, a subject quite as important to me as if I had been planning a million-dollar palace instead of a modest two-story, seven-room house on a fifty-foot lot. My life-long friend, several years older than I, had set out to give me proper instruction in home-building, and now he had brought me to this spacious, sleepy-looking settlement nestling between two cedar-clad ridges. The lawns were the triumphant product of the years, the trees along the street were giant elms, and everything about had that air of settled dignity that comes only with age.

"A house, like a human being, may be boastful, pretentious,

without good taste," my companion was saying, his voice slow and lazy in keeping with the drowsy afternoon, "and, as you spare no pains to avoid a man of that kind, so do you aim to shun such a house. Simplicity, the most beautiful quality in man or woman, is also the most beautiful quality in a home. And along with simplicity, permanence. The very spirit of the home, that which gives the word an appeal possessed by no other in our language, is the idea of permanence, and unless this idea is conveyed to the eye the creator of a home fails to attain beauty.

"I have traveled far in my day — more widely than most men, perhaps — and I have seen houses of human habitation in many lands, but I have never yet seen any material in which simplicity and permanence, the essentials of beauty, are so combined as in the brick. It has all the elements of a perfect building material, hardness, durability, imperviousness to moisture, non-conductivity of heat, adaptability to varied arrangement, convenience in handling. Fire, wind, rain, frost — all are helpless against it. It comes out of the Earth, and it is as indestructible as earth itself."

We stopped before the gap in a tall hedge, and peered through the shrubbery and trees at a rather small house of rich, dark brick. Its long side faced us, parallel with the road we were on, and it had an immaculate white entrance, decorated by two chaste columns, just opposite us in the middle; small-paned windows with white trimmings; and a white piazza at each end. Vines clung to it lovingly, and one corner was nearly hidden by a profusion of roses.

The building was simplicity itself. As it looked it did not occur to me to wonder what it had cost, whether five thousand or twenty thousand; and a minute later, when Huntington brought my thoughts back to practical things, I realized that this was a tribute to its perfect taste.

"It's almost irreverent to drag in the dollar mark in the presence of this," he said, "but, to use a phrase now made famous, 'you and I are practical men.' A builder of experience who saw that house would tell you that if the same plan had been carried out in frame the cost would have been only four or five hundred dollars less. You see what an effect the brick have given, what solidity and strength, what a faultless blend with the surrounding trees and grass and shrubbery. I venture to say the house is twenty years old if it's a day, yet it is more beautiful than when it was built, and the tone of it will become softer and mellower with every year that passes."

We saw many other homes that afternoon, of brick and of wood. And there were satisfying creations in both materials. But I noticed one thing that stayed in my mind a long time afterward: the frame houses that pleased the eye most were comparatively new, while the most beautiful of the brick houses were those that had reached a good old age. The one class was steadily depreciating, the other steadily improving, in appearance.

In the days that followed our stroll I made up for lost time by conducting a systematic investigation into building materials. Not only did I inquire into the practical business side, gathering statistics of original cost, maintenance, insurance and taxes, but I delved into the history of the various materials, and learned of their development in past centuries and in other lands than mine.

America has been the land of the frame house. The Pilgrim Fathers and those who followed them found forests seemingly inexhaustible, and the easiest and most inexpensive way for the settler to get stuff for his home was to shoulder an axe and attack the nearest clump of woods. His example was followed for three centuries, for the supply held out well, and not until a very few years ago did people come to see the clearer light, Unquestionably it was the economic factor that brought the truth out strong: the margin between the cost of indestructible brick and the cost of temporary frame approached closer and closer to the disappearing point. Then, when considerations of economy had forced brick upon the attention of home-builders, its architectural possibilities came to be studied and the discerning element in America awoke to an Ideal of Beauty that had been embraced long, long ago by the Old World.

In Europe rich and poor have built of brick for hundreds of years, and the traveler tells of brick homes that fit into the landscape as naturally as the streams and hills and trees themselves. If this happy result was possible in the past, it is even more so now. The advance in clay-burning methods has multiplied the colors and textures of brick; and this, with the progress achieved in producing varied shapes exactly as desired, has given to the designer the opportunity to attain that perfect harmony, in form and color, that is the acme of Beauty.

The Tale Of An Unbeliever.

SEVEN YEARS LATER—
"THE FORTRESS OF ROSES."

IT amuses me now when I recall the lectures I used to take from Huntington in those days just before my marriage. He showed little interest in the preparations for the Great Event—the ring I was to select, the gowns the bride and bridesmaids were to wear, and all that sort of thing — and he refused to be excited over the question whether the word "obey" should be included in the wife's oath. All his energies were concentrated upon persuading me to put up the proper kind of house. I remember with a deep feeling of gratitude how he stopped me on my mad career toward the choice of frame construction — how he made me think, and look about me, and ask questions.

At first I was inclined to laugh away his advice, but in the end he won; rather I won — by losing. During the period of these talks I wrote to my intended about them, and told her what Huntington said and what I answered; and I am forced to admit that she began to come around before I did. Woman's intuition, I suppose, pointed her to the right track.

Well, we deserted the frame construction idea and chose brick. It took considerable audacity, with our small available capital, even when we were convinced of the wisdom of it, but from the very moment of the decision we were glad. The brick were delivered promptly — almost anywhere nowadays you can get them without delay — and the construction proceeded smoothly to the end. In the same suburb half a dozen houses were going up then, and all around us we heard men grumbling about the poor quality of lumber and the difficulty of getting it promptly.

We used common brick for the main part of the walls and for the outer course an inexpensive, rather dark face brick that we had seen made up in sample panels. It produced an unobtrusive, soft-toned exterior; and the joints and uneven surfaces offer an ideal foothold for vines that we can see grow without fearing that they will rot our house away. Great clusters of roses make the piazza a bower. I swelled up proudly the other day when one of my fellow commuters lingered a moment before my door and said:

"Well, Temple, there are houses in this borough that cost five and ten times as much as yours, but not one is more pleasing to the eye."

And that is what continues to impress me most about brick, its adaptability to any financial condition. It is at once the most aristocratic and the most democratic of building materials — aristocratic because of its ancient supremacy, its dignity, and its defiance of attacks by time and the elements; democratic because of its plentifulness, its oneness with the earth we tread upon, and the ease with which any one of us, be he nabob or just safe from poverty, may possess it.

Now I am about to leave this sturdy little house in which we have lived so happily. Not because it failed to come up to expectations, for it more then fulfilled our hopes. But things have been going well with me in more ways than one; there are two children, and good fortune has come to me in my business. We must move into a larger place. There is no good reason against it, and many for it, yet I find myself almost resenting the prosperity that dictates the change.

Both of us kept finding excuses to put it off, after agreeing upon it last summer, and we might have been finding them yet if would-be purchasers had not crowded so thickly upon us. Two or three inviting offers we refused, but at last came one that we could not let pass, and the man is urging us to hurry out so that he can move in. He is paying us two thousand dollars more than our home cost. The rise in land values accounts for some of it, but the character of the house for most; only last month I heard the owner of a nearby frame house, put up at about the same time as mine, telling with great glee of selling for an advance of four hundred dollars. And I happen to know that he has laid out at least half that in repairing the building itself and frozen pipes.

There has been practically none of that in the "Fortress of Roses," as we nicknamed our home. The carpenter and the plumber are strangers to us. The brick walls, non-conductors of heat, have kept our rooms at least ten degrees cooler in summer than our neighbors and if the difference in winter had not been that much in our favor it is because they fed their furnaces far greater quantities of costly anthracite. And paint! Why, my wife and I would consider it nothing short of desecration to remove one trace of what the weather has done for the walls of the Fortress. While fellow suburbanites who have built of frame half a dozen years ago are studying colors and asking estimates from painters, our friends are continually telling us how our home, never yet painted and never to be, improves in appearance from year to year.

We have had a little demonstration, too, of what it means to have a fireproof home. The next house took fire in the night about two years ago, and the men who call themselves fire-fighting experts said afterward that all that saved us from serious damage was that the exposed wall was of brick. The dwelling on the other side got a bad scorching; the paint peeled off, and a frantic application of water, for two hours, was all that kept the boards from actually blazing.

When I look back over these short seven years it seems to me that my house has provided a perfect object lesson for young men who plan to build. It possesses all those qualities that should attach to the word home — strength, permanence, comfort, beauty — and the thought of leaving it brings a catch in the throat, as if I were parting forever from a near and dear friend. My only consolation is to vow, for the one hundredth or one thousandth time, that I will have for my new home the same variety of brick, and no other, that I see every evening when my flaxen-haired daughter meets me and leads me through the opening in the box hedge.

———

SUGGESTION FOR INTERIOR TREATMENT OF BUNGALOW

The Bungalow Indoors.

BY MARION GRIFFIN.

TO go through the doors of a Rhenish castle and find one-self in a Louis XV living-room is getting to be a stale joke. No matter how magnificent the building, this sort of thing is only indicative of sham, but it is the kind of monkey show we still see all about us and is the standard set even for the cottage. It shows a dishonesty so ingrained that we have almost lost our comprehension of the meaning of honesty. There is no more vestige of elegance in it than there is in the pirouettings and bowings and grimaces of a dog dressed up in petticoats with strings of pearls, running around on his hind legs on the vaudeville stage. Fortunately the "Bungalow" idea has brought with it a better sense of the congruous and the sense that the feeling, if not the materials, of the exterior should be brought within the house.

In a brick house the conformity of interior with exterior may be brought about in delightful ways. The same brick used in the outside walls may be used in the fireplace of the interior, and then the rich, soft minor tones, carried into the decorations, hangings and wall surfaces, result in most charming effects whether the brick be of unusual texture and color or the most common brick of the region; tones too that will stand any amount of sunlight without becoming garish, which will remain always restful to the eye and quieting to the nerves. For we are learning that color has a very positive effect on mood and temper, and should not leave to our schools alone the effort to take advantage of all external helps possible to comfort and inspiration.

There is a notion that brick cannot be used for interior walls without getting a feeling of coldness or publicity. This is not at all true, these results being entirely the consequence of the manner of handling. In some of the coziest and homiest rooms brick have been used for the walls as high as the head casing of doors and windows. By keeping these two features at the same level, we get a continuous line around the room dividing the height in pleasing proportions and making a natural line for the separation of materials.

The use of brick for this dado is particulaly appropriate in the children's playroom, doing away with the trying necessity of constant watchfulness or nagging to avoid defacement of surfaces.

Of course the desirability of using brick for sanitary purposes in the bath-rooms and kitchen is perfectly evident as is also the saving of effort on the part of the housekeeper and the saving of cost in renovation.

Honesty should lead us to use materials in accordance with their nature, and calls for highly intelligent research into their qualities and possibilities. The character of many of our rougher brick demands the elimination of high polish in the finish of wood to be used in connection with them, and moreover the beauty of the wood itself should lead us to keep it as nearly natural as is compatible with necessity for protection. All the woods are beautiful and only the aristocratic antipathy for the common can account for the commonplace, vulgar habit of imitating mahogany, for example, with red gum or birch.

The quality of each of the woods, matchless in its own way, can be preserved in its appropriate soft color and its delicate grain brought out by using a simple wax finish. In general the rugged lasting character of our house will be best conserved through the open-grained woods for the coarser brick with closer-grained woods for the smoother brick. And similarly in fabrics, while plain surfaces should predominate throughout, the textures should correspond in character with the brick.

In our hangings let us avoid the incongruity of white lace curtains with their delicate mesh and dainty motives, and where we want sash curtains have them in keeping by using straight falls of some low-toned material like some of the Kentucky linens, or screen scrim, or other simple net.

For carpets, in the fluff rugs made from old ingrain carpets, we can get very suitable coverings most economical and entirely in harmony with the other materials we are considering and very beautiful in themselves. By selection, rugs of uniform tone can be obtained, than which nothing better is to be found.

Nothing is more trying to our nerves or displeasing to the eye than to have a lot of heterogeneous motives huddled together; for a design is an expression of an emotion and the jarring effect of a lot of indiscriminate visual motives is quite as great though not at present so clearly understood as would be the throwing together of snatches of music of different character as pastoral, and jig, and hymn and dirge.

The confusion to which we doom ourselves when we use figured wall papers, figured rugs, figured curtains, figured upholstery, is responsible for much of the weariness of the women who spend so much of their time in the house, for peevishness of children who cannot be expected to understand the causes of their discomfort, and for grouchiness of men who need rest when they come home from a days' work, who would resent being obliged to listen to discordant notes constantly jangling in their ears, and if sufficiently intelligent to understand the cause of their discomfort would resent being subjected to discordant visual notes.

SUGGESTION FOR INTERIOR TREATMENT OF BUNGALOW

We understand this fact of harmony or discord in music. In the course of the centuries it finally dawned on us that there was a law in accordance with which sounds were pleasing or displeaasing to us. We studied into the nature of the law and then we entered into the great, new, limitless world of music — a heaven of measureless delights.

A building is line, form, motive, and until we realize that they must be used in conformity to law to be pleasing we will get occasional satisfying results but no great or growing architecture, and as all things act and react on each other so the very development of our character—our souls, is dependent on these laws of nature which are spiritual as well as physical in themselves and in their effects.

The necessities of the small house holder are totally different from those of larger establishments and the introduction of elements which are most convenient in the latter case into the former problem, resulting from lack of realization of the difference in the problem, often leads to waste, extravagance and actual inconvenience.

In the bungalow where one does one's own work or at most employs one assistant, added steps, inconvenience in getting at implements and materials and waste of space should be avoided. A small kitchen properly arranged with cupboards on the walls is not only an economy in building but a most desirable arrangement for the housekeeper. When we stop to think what meals can be turned out of the tiny kitchen of a dining-car we are brought to a realizing sense of the wastefulness and inconvenience of our ordinary domestic arrangements.

Again, the space used for hall and stairways in a large house are unnecessary in a bungalow. The plan should be so arranged that in a compact and restricted area access can be given to all the various parts of the house as entrance, living-room, kitchen and second story, while maintaining the privacy of each and avoiding making a thoroughfare of any. The grand stairway, appropriate enough in a palace with its functions of pomp and parade, becomes an absurdity in our domestic life — a manner of living totally unknown two centuries ago.

The flexibility of a small house is much increased by throwing the living-rooms together so far as possible, for no matter how small the family there are many times when for social purposes it is necessary to have a large room. Nor does this arrangement interfere with the proper fulfiling of the separate functions of living and dining-room, for the nature of these two rooms is such that when one of them is occupied the other is empty. The economy of throwing the space of the two together is obvious. The necessity of separating guests from the confusion of elaborate service does not exist. Such separation of dining-table from living quarters as might oc-

View in Living-Dining Room

SUGGESTION FOR INTERIOR TREATMENT OF BUNGALOW

casionally be needed can be easily effected by the use of a screen. On festival occasions the whole space can serve as dining-room, arranged with tables which can be easily removed, leaving a fine big room for frolic when the feast is done. Indeed I have known very small houses that could entertain on a much larger scale than really big ones, simply as a consequence of a well-thought out plan.

Small rooms, each capable of being cut off from the others, is an arrangement no longer necessary. The old difficulties of heating and housekeeping which made it easier to keep one room immaculate, ready for the reception of the occasional guest, have been done away with. We live too close to each other in these days, too intimately, on too democratic a footing to make us wish to have a little show spot. We open our homes as our hearts and are not ashamed of our occupations. It is no doubt convenient to have one room, call it reception room or den or grouch or study or office, where seclusion is possible, but under ordinary circumstances this need is subordinate to the more constant and pressing needs of our every-day life. More and more we are becoming conscious of the value of harmonizing and unifying the interests of all the members of a family, men and women, old and young — a movement which is permeating all our community where opportunity in education and business is unifying the social life of all.